Moralism and
Politics and Di

THE CREDIBILITY OF INSTITUTIONS, POLICIES AND LEADERSHIP
A Series funded by the Hewlett Foundation
Kenneth W. Thompson, *Series Editor*

I. Ideas and Approaches to Politics and Foreign Policy

Volume 1: Moralism and Morality in Politics and Diplomacy
Kenneth W. Thompson

Volume 2: The American Approach to Foreign Policy: A Pragmatic Perspective
Cecil V. Crabb, Jr.

Volume 3: Functionalism and Interdependence
John Eastby

Volume 4: American Approaches to World Affairs
I. L. Claude

II. Institutions and Public Attitudes

Volume 5: The Media
Kenneth W. Thompson (ed.)

Volume 6: The Private Sector
J. Wilson Newman

Volume 7: The President and the Public: Rhetoric and National Leadership
Kathy B. and Craig Allen Smith (eds.)

Volume 8: Law and Diplomacy: The Plimpton Papers
Mrs. Francis T.P. Plimpton

Volume 9: Bureaucracy and Statesmanship
Robert A. Strong

III. Consensus and Public Policy

Volume 10: The Last European Peace Conference: Paris 1946— Conflict of Values
Stephen Kertesz

Volume 11: Foreign Policy and Domestic Consensus
Richard Melanson and Kenneth W. Thompson (eds.)

Volume 12: Consensus: Issues and Problems
Michael Joseph Smith and Kenneth W. Thompson (eds.)

Volume 13: McCarthyism and Consensus?
William B. Ewald, Jr.

Volume 14: Consensus and the American Mission
Brian Klunk

Volume 15: The United States Acquires the Philippines: Consensus vs. Reality
Louis J. Halle

IV. Leaders and Credibility

Volume 16: Essays on Leadership: Comparative Insights
Kenneth W. Thompson (ed.)

Volume 17: American Moral and Political Leadership in the Third World
Kenneth W. Thompson (ed).

Volume 18: U.S. Leadership in Asia and the Middle East
Kenneth W. Thompson (ed.)

Volume 19: Winston S. Churchill: Philosopher and Statesman
Michael Fowler

Volume 20: Institutions and Leadership: Prospects for the Future
Kenneth W. Thompson (ed.)

Moralism and Morality in Politics and Diplomacy

The Credibility of Institutions, Policies and Leadership
Volume 1

Kenneth W. Thompson

University Press of America
Lanham • New York • London

Copyright © 1985 by

University Press of America,™ Inc.

4720 Boston Way
Lanham, MD 20706

3 Henrietta Street
London WC2E 8LU England

Co-published by arrangement with
The White Burkett Miller Center of Public Affairs,
University of Virginia

Library of Congress Cataloging in Publication Data

Thompson, Kenneth W., 1921-
  Moralism and morality in politics and diplomacy.

  1. International relations—Moral and ethical aspects.
I. Title.
JX1255.T46   1985   172'.4   84-27000
ISBN 0-8191-4424-X (alk. paper)
ISBN 0-8191-4425-8 (pbk. : alk. paper)

Contents

Introduction

With the publication of Kenneth W. Thompson's *Moralism and Morality in Politics and Diplomacy,* the White Burkett Miller Center of Public Affairs' launches a new series on "The Credibility of Leadership and Institutions" made possible through the assistance of the William and Flora Hewlett Foundation.

In seeking to understand the trust or lack of trust of Americans in their political and social institutions and in the resulting policies, the series is being organized under four major headings:

1. Philosophical Approaches to Politics and Foreign Policy
2. The Obsolescence and Durability of Institutions
3. Policy Case Studies in Consensus and Dissensus
4. Leadership: the United States and Abroad

Each theme will be explored from at least two different perspectives by two individual authors. Companion volumes to the present study of moralism and morality as a philosophical approach include inquiries into pragmatism, functionalism and interdependence and studies of realism and idealism.

In the area of policy case studies, a group of scholars and policymakers will revisit the great era of consensus in American foreign policy from 1946 to 1949 in which major responses to postwar Soviet expansionism were forged. The Truman Doctrine, Marshall Plan and NATO represent the high water mark in public agreement over ends and means in the Cold War and in the successful implementation of a policy of containment. The breakdown in consensus occurred with the Vietnam War. In comparing the historic policies of the Truman administration with American policies in Vietnam, the requirements of consensus for policy will be examined and evaluated.

Further, for more than a half century, attitudes toward some of our most basic social institutions have been in flux. For the present or future, it is difficult if not impossible to assess the durability of particular institutions. Social science measures of the degree and extent of change are imperfect. Observers and critics differ on their future. Some institutions may be in decline and are likely to be replaced yet other observers argue that our leading institutions have never been more healthy and therefore deserve public confidence and support. It is the purpose of the Hewlett Series to evaluate the sources of strength or weakness of particular institutions, including the mass media, the church, the private sector, and the state. Studies are being organized to ask whether the problems of leading institutions result from the same causes or whether the rise and fall of each social institution is unique.

If public confidence in policies and institutions is difficult to evaluate, public trust in American leaders is even more complex. A curious and intangible nexus of trust or mistrust links the public and its leaders. We understand the popularity of a four-term president, Franklin D. Roosevelt, but are less clear why one president retains popularity into his fourth year while another lost his early in an administration. Moreover, cultures shape conditions under which some leaders gain and hold public trust and other are unable to attain such trust. By examining leadership at home and abroad, the new Series may help isolate and define some of the elements and variables producing trust in leadership in widely different cultures.

The first four volumes in the Series deal with certain dominant views of politics and world affairs. We are especially concerned with the question of the understanding Americans have of such philosophies and the use they make of them in the policies they espouse. How fully do they grasp the underlying principles of morality or pragmatism or other leading theories as the basis for action and policymaking? Does the public use theories to guide their comprehension of politics? We are concerned, both with ideas and approaches and with the public's perception of ideas.

Finally, it is the purpose of our discussion of four different philosophies of politics to help students and citizens to distinguish the main differences in thought and action, say, between moralism and morality or pragmatism and functionalism. The four approaches are widely used but less often examined in careful and critical studies such as are projected in the Hewlett Series.

PART ONE

The Philosophical Issues

Moralism, Morality and Politics: Ultimate Standards Vs. a Strategy of Success

Political and moral theorists confront no more agonizing question than the evaluation of morality measured against the strategy of success. It seems fitting at the outset of the inquiry to ask what can we say about the relationship of ultimate standards of right and wrong and political success.

1. MORALISM AND CYNICISM

One way to open our discussion is to question whether either of the most popular and prevailing viewpoints concerning this relationship can stand scrutiny and criticism. One outlook which is particularly attractive to some religious and self-consciously moral people sees the virtuous as being rewarded here and now. Goodness and success are equated. Quite understandably, hardpressed men and nations seek comfort in a troubled world; some find it in the promises of a positive faith. It is observable that leaders who tie their star to particular religious spokesmen, defenders of a popular political faith, gain certain political advantages. Moral fervor, whether directly or indirectly expressed, has its compensations. What could be more natural and in keeping with the culture than a belief that the strivings of the visibly pious and self-proclaimed leader will be sanctified by house theologians or celebrated in public approbation. Morality in this sense can be said to be good politics. Morality = success. Or moralism?

By contrast, the opposite view of morality and success is a version of Leo Duroscher's more than slightly cynical and fatalistic proposition that "good guys finish last." Not only does morality not guarantee success but in some political contests stands in the way. The operational political test is skill in organizing political power to achieve one's ends. It is the ability to take command and to control the situation. For moral man in a immoral society, something more than a simple morality is required in politics. The political leader must have the ability to build coalitions, form new balances of power and cope with persistent realities. It is an escape from politics to preach morality and not recognize the need to influence and coerce, critics say.

Yet critics of moralism and cynicism apparently speak with more authority in intellectual than in popular discourse for in one form or another these two viewpoints continue to dominate politics and public discussions of politics. For the man in the street, politics more often than not is depicted as the good man rising above the crowd or the sinister man playing the dirty game of politics. Many Americans prefer the halo or the sneer. We have visions of the moral man elevating the level of politics when we say President "X" is not one of the Washington crowd. It is no accident that successful presidential candidates in recent campaigns have run against official Washington. To succeed they have sought to hold up their virtue and compare it with that of more experienced hence tarnished politicians.

In the opposing camp, those whose vision of politics never goes beyond emphasizing wheeling and dealing scoff at writers who claim for any national leader praiseworthy strengths and qualities. Cynics are the great debunkers and for them the discovery that Abraham Lincoln as a young legislator padded his expense account is more noteworthy than the message of the Gettysburg Address. Cynics are the revisionists who cut respected leaders down to size. If moralists exaggerate virtue in political life, cynics seek to destroy it. Both suffer from the consequences of having thrown all balance and moderation to the wind. If the two perspectives are the sole alternative for thinking about morality and politics, we are in a bad way. Fortunately other perspectives exist and gain strength from the excesses of the two approaches. Let us turn now to explore them as they have appeared in part as a reaction to moralism and cynicism.

2. MORALISM AND MORALITY IN DEMOCRACIES

A nation, particularly a democratic nation and especially the United States tends to view its actions as taking place within a moral framework. On one hand, it sees itself as subject to certain moral limitations, restraints and judgments; on the other, it looks to national goals and historic traditions as the explanation and moral justification for its course of action. Seldom if ever is foreign policy defended by arguing for the maintenance or increase of national power or of national survival. Rather Americans and other nationals speak of standing for moral purposes beyond the state: democracy or communism, freedom or equality, order or justice and historical inevitability. Whatever cynics may say, foreign policy tends to be articulated in moral terms, even in most authoritarian regimes, whether those terms be social justice, economic equality, the overthrow of colonialism, national liberation or putting an end to an unjust status quo.

To know that men and nations espouse goals and ends that transcend national defense or survival is a first step or approach but not a solution to the moral problem. In fact, it is more a claim than an approach; it may bespeak what George F. Kennan and Hans J. Morgenthau have called moralism as distinguished from morality. Moralism is the tendency to make one moral value supreme and to apply it indiscriminately without regard to time and place; morality by comparison is the endless quest for what is right amidst the complexity of competing and sometimes conflicting, sometimes compatible moral ends. Professor Paul Freund of the Harvard Law School centered his 1976 Thomas Jefferson Memorial Lecture of the National Endowment for the Humanities on Lord Acton's aphorism: "when you perceive a truth, look for a balancing truth." According to Freund, we suffer in western civilization from the decline of the ancient art of moral reasoning, the essence of which is weighing and balancing not only good and evil but competing "goods."

Freedom and order, liberty and justice, economic growth and social equality, national interest and the well-being of mankind are each in themselves worthy moral ends. How much simpler moral choice would be if the leader could select one value as his guiding principle and ignore all the rest. In every human community, however, the choice between right and wrong is endlessly fraught with complexity and grounded in deep moral pathos. There is an inescapably tragic character to moral choice. Within the family, men all too often may be driven to choose between family interests and professional responsibilities, between devotion to one and neglect of the other, between too much of one and too little of the other. Loyalty to spouse and children may conflict with caring for aging parents. Within the nation, freedom of speech and assembly may clash with the requirements of security and order. The Supreme Court has declared that freedom of speech does not involve the right to cry fire in a crowded theatre. The right to a fair trial may collide with the right to know and the freedom of the press. Freedom of scientific inquiry apparently does not justify the right of a graduate student to produce a nuclear bomb in his kitchen. Even within the most developed democracy every political and constitutional principle coexists and is related to every other principle, and each is at most a partial expression of morality; for as Reinhold Niebuhr wrote: "Democracy cannot exist if there is no recognition of the fragmentary character of all systems of values which are allowed to exist within its frame."

Within the family and the democratic nation, however, forces are at work to protect fragmentary values and interests, to hold moral absolution in check and to prevent men from erecting a single principle into an all-controlling moral dogma. The rights of individuals are weighed against the rights of the group. Society has long-established procedures and institutions through which claims and counter-claims are weighed and adjudicated. A vast panoply of political and constitutional rights and instruments of social legislation are invoked to prevent abuses that threaten the weakest elements of society, including minorities and the powerless, little children, the infirm and the aged. The law of love which lies beyond the reach of large collectivities (political parties do not love one another) is at least theoretically a practical possibility within the family. Even within the family, however, some form of distributive justice may prove to be man's highest moral attainment, as many loving husbands and wives or devoted parents and children will attest. Justice within the family involves giving each party its due and often this is as much a matter of calculating needs and interests as of pure and unselfish love.

Within the nation, the Bill of Rights and the American Constitutional system provide a means of mediating justice for individuals and groups, minorities and majorities, the weak and the strong. As love is mediated through justice in the family, the "Higher Law" principles on which the Constitution is based support the unending quest for rights within American society. The health of democracy rests finally on the possibility of minorities becoming majorities, on some approximation of justice and on a common sense recognition that no single value or principle is a final guide to moral rectitude. In Niebuhr's words:

> The triumph of common sense is . . . primarily the wisdom of democracy itself which prevents [anyone's] strategy from being carried through to its logical conclusion. There is an element of truth in each position which becomes falsehood precisely when it is carried through too consistently.

3. MORALISM AND MORALITY IN INTERNATIONAL POLITICS

The moral problem as exemplified within the family and within democratic nations is more readily comprehended and understood than for the fragile and embryonic community of nations. More than one hundred and sixty nations make up international society, each with its own political and economic system, institutions and practices, needs and traditions. Each has its own requirements of governance, its necessities of state and its own rights and restraints inherent in its political order. For manifold reasons, the moral problem for politics among nation states is more complex than for families and democracies. The first duty of any national statesman is preservation of the union—a requirement that both limits his actions and directs some of them along lines that are offensive to ideas of personal morality. President Lincoln pointed out in his letter to Horace Greeley that "My primary purpose is to save the Union." If this meant freeing all the slaves he would do so or none of the slaves he would do so or freeing some but not others he would do so. His choice from the standpoint of national morality was not necessarily the choice he would have made from the standpoint of personal morality. Nor could he assure national unity without paying homage to domestic political realities. Louis Halle has written:

Lincoln, in his Emancipation Proclamation, excluded the slaves in certain states because he needed the support of the congressmen from those states. This exclusion, although morally reprehensible in itself, made possible the eventual emancipation of all the slaves. I hold that the moralists who denounced him for this immoral act of expediency were wrong.

The demands of statecraft are sometimes more severe even than Lincoln's choice, prompting the words of the Italian nationalist, Cavour: "If we had done for ourselves what we did for the state what scoundrels we would be." One remembers the classical definition of the diplomat as "a man sent abroad to lie and deceive in the interests of the state" amended by the late Harold Nicolson who wrote: "Yes, but he must also return to negotiate another day." We are reminded of Niebuhr's *Moral Man and Immoral Society* and we are reminded also of his warning that realists are forever threatened by the temptation of cynicism.

The crux of the matter is that foreign policy, as viewed by most students of diplomacy, is conducted by governments, as a function of their governmental responsibility; it must serve the purposes of governments generally; "its primary purpose must be is preservation of the union" (Lincoln) informed by the national interest and the dictates of national security. Yet the outspoken champion of political realism, Hans J. Morgenthau, argued that the conduct of foreign policy is not devoid of moral significance. Political actors come under moral judgment and witness to the values of their societies. However, the overall environment today of international politics is marked both by moral improvement and retrogression. There have been advances in respect for human life since the 15th and 16th centuries when, for example, the Republic of Venice carried on its rolls an official poisoner whose continued employment depended on his success in disposing of the leaders of adversary states. Compare this with the sharp moral indignation of Winston S. Churchill when Stalin at Teheran proposed, half mockingly but not wholly in jest, that 50,000 German leaders be summarily shot to put an end to the threat of future German aggression. Or contrast it with the force of public reaction in the United States to disclosures concerning possible plans for political assassinations by the CIA.

Yet in other sectors the international scene witnesses to the decline of international morality, indicating that moral restraints are weakening if not disappearing in distinctions in wartime between combattants and non-combattants. According to the Hague Convention of 1899 and 1907, only soldiers ready to fight were considered combattants and objects of war, but by World War II this distinction had effectively been obliterated in the saturation bombings in which both sides engaged. The international environment, therefore, was marked by a decline in international morality brought about in part by the technology of warfare and in part by a diminution of standards concerning the sanctity of human life. In war and peace, therefore, the world has seen moral improvement in some spheres but a decline in others resulting from the fact that universal moral principles which are omnipresent are filtered through circumstances of time and place and through national concepts determining their application. In peace, there remains an enormous gap between, say, American respect for the elemental principle of respect for human life and refusal to take human life except in extraordinary circumstances (capital punishment, abortion, euthanasia and other carefully defined and delimited exceptions) and the much less strict constraints in other civilizations which have been far more extravagant in taking human life for political and ideological purposes (Stalin and the Kulaks, Hitler and the Jews and the punishment of thieves in Saudi Arabia by cutting off their hands). The relation of universal principles to time and circumstances and to the culture and necessities of different nations and contemporary civilizations has been controlling. Particular moral imperatives are obeyed by particular nations at particular times and not by others, and this is the overarching characteristic of today's international environment.

Moralists are inclined to see only the gains and advances in international society, particularly those appropriate to their ends, whereas cynics, pointing to the struggle in which the adversary lies, cheats and steals, excuse themselves by invoking necessity for acting as if the whole international order was without rules or standards as in the mining without warning of the harbor in Nicaragua in 1984.

On January 28, 1977, Carter wrote in his diary: "Everybody has warned me not to take on too many projects so early in the administration, but its almost impossible to delay something that I see needs to be done" (*Keeping Faith,* p. 65). If Carter faltered and stumbled as President it was not because of the nobility of his ends. His failures occurred in the realm of means. He found it difficult to fix priorities. It was not in his nature to bargain and horsetrade with congressmen and party leaders. He found it burdensome if not offensive. To this day, Carter has never understood the high price he paid for having two secretaries of state, two voices in American foreign policy. Despite his love for all mankind, he had difficulty remembering the names of younger subordinates, including some junior associates with whom he worked closely.

It is fair to ask what impact Carter's faith had on his decision-making. That his faith was deep and constant, few who know him best would question. Throughout his presidency, he continued whenever possible to teach Sunday School. He made no secret of being a "born again Christian." Yet he sought not to inject religion into politics for partisan advantage. What influence it had on his decisionmaking is admittedly speculative. In one respect, it undoubtedly fortified and strengthened him. In another [he prayed a lot], his particular religious outlook may have led him to absolutize moral and political goals. Years later in 1982 in an oral history conducted by the Miller Center, Carter acknowledged he had not recognized the sharp conflict that existed at times between the goal of human rights and the achievement of a SALT II agreement with the Russians. He may also not have seen that his concerted effort in the first year or two to achieve a Panama Canal agreement diverted administration energy from pursuing SALT II negotiations to an early conclusion. His most notable foreign policy achievement came when at Camp David he abandoned his negative view toward quiet diplomacy, born during the campaign and spawned partly by Brzezinski's rivalry with Henry Kissinger. After thirteen days on the mountain with all reporters excluded, Carter, Menachem Begin and Anwar el-Sadat signed an agreement that many consider the high point of the Carter presidency. It was a triumph of persistence, careful preparation and personal resolve demonstrating that President Carter did have capacities to succeed in the realm of means.

What remains the principal puzzle of the Carter presidency is how a leader with so much passion for detail could falter primarily where means were involved. Perhaps the answer, if there is an answer, will appear when historians disentangle the relationship between the goals of this highly religious man who could often be moralistic and the methods he employed to achieve his ends. It could be that somewhere on the road to the presidency, Carter forgot what Reinhold Niebuhr wrote that politics is the point where conscience and power meet and political choices always involve compromises between the morally desirable and the politically possible. He may not have learned from Niebuhr the need for prudence, practical morality and moral reasoning. His moralism may have opened the door to the cynicism of his successor. Any President engages in backing and filling but the distance between his Notre Dame speech promising Americans he would free them from the inordinate fear of communism and his turnabout and actions after Afghanistan was excessive. The twin perils of moralism are its unwillingness to measure all the possible consequences of pursuing noble ends and its surprise when events turn disappointed moralists into disillusioned cynics.

4. THE PERSISTENCE OF MORALISM AND CYNICISM

To sum up, moralism and cynicism come together in recent American foreign policy propelled by the expectation of success. One administration prophesies world leadership resulting from a crusade to demonstrate America's renewed righteousness after Watergate. The other offers moral and political supremacy through military superiority. Both neglect Niebuhr's warning:

> The more we indulge in an uncritical reverence for the supposed wisdom of our American way of life, the more odious we make it in the eyes of the world, and the more we destroy our moral authority, without which our economic and military power will become impotent. Thus we are undermining the reality of our power by our uncritical pride in it.

Yet recent administrations, however well-intentioned, have ignored such warnings, the one by imagining that an American human rights campaign would find universal acceptance around the world and the other in supposing that a display of expanding military power would bring down opposing political systems and

install American political values. What is it in the American culture that so easily turns quite different political groups away from
prudent judgments to the moralistic approach? It will not do or be
persuasive to point only to one or two elements of the national life.
Moralism is deeply rooted and its sources are many and not one. It
may help to enumerate some of them.

One source of moralism is the uniqueness of America's position in the world from its founding through the early 20th century.
Not only were its beginnings ones in which Americans saw themselves as a chosen people and a city on a hill but the European
balance of power and the British navy served to protect the new
nation's security. The United States saw itself as a chosen people
freed from the toils of European power politics. American ex-
ceptionalism was explained largely as the outcome of moral
superiority, not the result of a favored geographical position. If the
authors of the *Federalist Papers* were more discerning, the
panpheteers and preachers were not. Morally, the nation was not
like other nations and its freedom from foreign intervention was a
product of its virtue.

More than a century later, Woodrow Wilson sought to bring
the new freedom to the world. The gains of one nation united in
freedom under God was the legacy that Wilson offered to the rest
of the world. National self-determination which had given peace to
the Western Hemisphere promised universal peace once established throughout the world. Before and after World War II, the
mission was to create a worldwide federal union patterned after
the union of the thirteen states which was merely a "great rehearsal"
for unity in the world. Most Americans assumed that the success
of constitutionalism for them was a reflection of unique moral
strengths. With these and other examples what is striking is the
consistency with which American morality and success were linked
for Americans.

Finally, moralism has often been good politics and some political leaders have turned to it instinctively not without a touch of
cynicism. Apparently, it is a national trait to wish to cover harsh
political truths with a cloak of righteousness. From another
standpoint, this fact may account in part at least for the more
sweeping reaction of Americans than Europeans to moral and
political abuses such as Watergate, although Nixon in that action
may have crossed what Niebuhr chose to call the moral threshold.

It has always been difficult to separate moralism and politics in the United States. There is a close and intimate link between the two especially in political rhetoric. It sets us apart from cultures in which morality is seen as the result of moral reasoning and of weighing competing goods and practical possibilities. It breaks the ties of present day politics with that of the Founding Fathers.

Then of course there is the force of the mass media. Every successful politician knows the importance of simplification especially in the electronic age. Thus the tendency of moralists to reduce moral truth to one or two moral principles fits the demands of modern communication like a glove. Thus moralism and communication in politics march together in our age.

But to conclude this part of our inquiry on a more positive note, western thought and notably Judeo-Christian thought particularly in its more profound expressions, offers an alternative to moralism measured by success. That alternative is a safeguard to the tendency of moralism to spill over into cynicism, disillusionment and despair. It rests on a two tiered concept of morality: first, that of ultimate standards such as love and justice which inspire and drive human goodness and virtue but are never fully realized or exhausted in practice (Niebuhr condemned those who sought to make a success story out of the cross); and second, moral reasoning which understands that practical moral judgments are an unending process of weighing competing moral goods: freedom and equality, order and justice, national security and global survival. Oliver Wendell Holmes said that "some people admire the man of principle. I admire the man who can find his way through a maze of conflicting moral principles." Prudence in politics involves the balancing, if not the reconciling, of what is morally desirable with what is politically possible. Lincoln was a sad man, John F. Kennedy said, because he discovered that in politics you can't have everything. Moralists and cynics alike reject this view, moralists because often they *do* want everything, cynics because they doubt anything is enough worth having to warrant the struggle.[1]

NOTES

1. This chapter is a modified version of the Stuber Lectures delivered at the University of Rochester on May 14-15, 1984.

The Ethical Dimensions of Diplomacy

KENNETH W. THOMPSON

William Graham Summer wrote: "The amount of superstition is not much changed, but it now attaches to politics, not to religion." For politics, the present observer would substitute diplomacy. In ancient societies, men called on the gods to rid their world of evil, conflict and suffering. If war persisted, they asked the gods to reward their side with victory. What men in their frailty could not accomplish, the gods would provide. They would protect the weak and reward virtue. If men could not bring justice into the social order, the gods would assure that justice was done. From ancient tribal deities to the gods who presided over the knights of the roundtable, their task ultimately was to smooth out the troubled path along which heroic men had to walk.

An opposing view of morality is rooted in classical traditions and certain historic versions of the Judaeo-Christian faith. It is true that some moralists, nationalists and religiously oriented people are tempted to make a success story out of their faith. Yet no one, and least of all religious leaders, can guarantee prosperity and success, even though certain early religious movements in the colonies and thirteen states sought to demonstrate that outer signs of well-being pointed in the direction of inner virtue. The twentieth century theologian, Reinhold Niebuhr wrote of two men, one who tithed from his youth and gained great wealth. That man explained his success as deriving from his lifelong observance of religious practices. The other man, Adam Denger, by whom the young Niebuhr was employed in a grocery store in Lincoln, Illinois, generously extended credit to miners who had lost their jobs. However the miners left Lincoln without paying their debts and their benefactor was destroyed. In her biography of Niebuhr, June

Bingham writes: "Mr. Denger kept believing that God would protect him if he did what was right. But God let Adam Denger go bankrupt and his young assistant grew up to preach against sentimentality and reliance on special providence."[1] When Niebuhr preached against the self-serving views of those who proclaimed that God would reward them, he chose as his text the Biblical passage: "For He makes his sun rise on the evil and the good and sends rain on the just and unjust." Nothing in scripture assures that the virtuous will always gain success or that the righteous will inherit wealth and riches. According to Niebuhr, it is a corruption of religion to hold out the promise that the good man or the virtuous nation will always be triumphant or that evil empires will be destroyed. Religious people too often are found lobbying in the courts of the Almighty proclaiming their goodness and offering their piety as proof that they deserve special favors. A more profound understanding of man and God would emphasize the tragic element in history. The unending process in diplomacy of balancing the forces of harmony and disharmony is at war with the notion that those who are good and virtuous are destined through some form of divine intervention to inherit prosperity and success.

A more contemporary version of the intrusion of false and superstitious notions about ethics and diplomacy is what Louis J. Halle has called "Pharisaism." He asserts that posturing by those who claim to be more virtuous than their fellow men is not true morality. In the parable of the Pharisee and the publican (Luke 18:10–14), those who make ostentatious display of their morality striking moralistic poses and pointing to the iniquity of others are condemned for their false morality. Politicians and diplomats who are overwhelmingly concerned with the morality of others ought as a rule to be mistrusted. By their attitudes, they would have others believe they have achieved so complete a level of morality they are qualified to judge others. They depend not on the gods for their morality but on their own supposed moral perfection.

Another version of morality is that of Manicheism which portrays the world in radical terms of absolute good and evil or right and wrong. Americans are predisposed to a form of Manicheism by childhood distinctions between good guys and bad guys or cops and robbers. The false logic of Manicheism lies at the heart of every crusading ideology and of civilization's long record, ever since the wars of religion, of unspeakable brutalities of one people against another. In the end, Manicheism becomes a negative morality based on punishment and retribution. According to the mythology of Manicheism, a particular group or class is seen as a Satanic evil. For the Germans the Jews, for the allies the Germans and Japanese, for the bourgeoisie the communists and for the communists the bourgeoisie are the one evil force in the world. Once that evil has been rooted out and eradicated, peace and harmony will prevail. Not by accident, Khomeini depicts the United States as the Great Satan in what is but the most recent form of Manicheism. Those who belong to groups who for others personify evil may in the name of morality be chastised or destroyed in order that justice be done.

A final version of morality identifies the good with the novel and the changing and evil with continuity and past practices. Since the end of the Napoleonic Wars, ever larger groups of Western leaders have denounced diplomacy and international politics as an unhappy stage in the progress of mankind that was bound to disappear once the particular historical circumstances that gave rise to it had been transformed. European diplomacy was an archaism that history would eliminate when reason and morality prevailed. For some writers, a particular social evil caused the corruption of international society: colonies for Jeremy Bentham, trade barriers for Cobden and Proudhon, capitalism for Marx and the absence of self-government for liberals. It was Richard Cobden who declared: "At some future election, we may probably see the test 'no foreign politics' applied to those who offer to become the representatives of free constituencies."[2] After World War I, the Nye Committee in 1934–36 investigated on behalf of the United States Senate the role of certain financial and industrial interests suspected of having been responsible for the entry of the United States into that war. Not the requirements of the national interest but certain self-seeking groups who profited from the war were thought to have been responsible for our involvement. Manufacturers of war materiel and international bankers had lured the nations into war. According to this devil theory, a handful of war profiteers and munition makers were responsible for war. If the nation could rid itself of their conspiratorial and nefarious influence, peace would prevail.

In a similar vein, others saw in European diplomacy and power politics the cause of all conflict. In 1943, Secretary of State Cordell Hull on returning from the Moscow Conference, which prepared the way for the creation of the United Nations, proclaimed that the new international organization would lead to the end of power politics which had ravaged European society. Earlier President Woodrow Wilson, prematurely as history was to demonstrate, prophesied that the common interests of mankind were replacing national interests. In 1946, the British Minister of State, Philip Noel-Baker, stood in the House of Commons to say that his government was "determined to use the institutions of the United Nations to kill power politics, in order that, by the methods of democracy, the will of the people shall prevail."[3]

Underlying all those views is the conviction that a certain group or a particular social and international order represent evil forces which alone are responsible for the immorality of diplomacy and politics. The path to a moral international order is one along which these evil forces will be made to disappear. Once they are rooted out, an ethical international system will be assured and conflict will come to an end.

1. HUMAN NATURE AND DIPLOMACY

Opposed to the essentially utopian views of the several versions of morality and diplomacy discussed above is another conception of human nature and diplomacy. According to this perspective, human nature has not changed since the days of classical antiquity. Man is both good and evil and his virtues and vices persist no less in a technologically advanced than a primitive society. Politics and diplomacy bring out the harshest side of man's nature. Thucydides is therefore, as Hobbes declared in another age, "the most Politick Historiographer that ever lived." The Melian dialogue has relevance even in an age of interdependence. Melos had remained neutral during the war between Sparta and Athens but the Athenians, during a long truce, confronted them with an expeditionary force calling on them to join the Athenian alliance or be exterminated. When the Melians resist, Thucydides reports the ensuing dialogue. The Athenians explain that justice depends upon the power to compel; the strong do what they have the power to do and the weak accept what they must. Even the gods will not help because they behave toward one another and toward men as the Athenians plan to behave toward Melos. The Athenians conclude: "It is a general and necessary law of nature to rule wherever one can. This is not a law we made ourselves, nor were we the first to act on it when it was made. We found it already in existence, and we shall leave it to exist forever among those who come after us." Melos resists and is destroyed.

Frederick the Great in his *Origin of the Bismarck Policy* or *The Hohenzollern Doctrine and Maxims,* written for his successor to the throne, summarizes his opinions on religion, morals, politics and diplomacy saying: "We monarchs take what we can, when we can, and we are never in the wrong, except when compelled to give up what we had taken."[4] Of religion, Frederick wrote: "Religion is absolutely necessary in a State government. . . . [But] there is nothing which tyrannizes over the mind and heart so much as religion, because it agrees neither with our passions, nor with the high political views which a monarch should entertain. . . . When he is about to conclude a treaty with some foreign power, if he only remembers that he is a Christian, all is lost: he will always suffer himself to be duped or imposed upon."[5] Frederick defended the right of each religious sect to pray and seek salvation as they wished but found they were destined never to agree. Of justice, Frederick declared: "We owe justice to our subjects as they owe us respect . . . but it is necessary to take care that we are not brought under subjection by justice itself."[6] For Frederick: "Justice is the image of God. Who can therefore attain to so high a perfection."[7] "Behold all the countries in the world, and examine if justice is administered exactly in the same manner."[8] What troubled Frederick most was that if the trends he observed continued, one-tenth of the kingdom's subjects in the next century would be engaged in the administration of justice with "that sure and steady way of proceeding which lawyers have . . . [and] that clever manner of preserving their advantages under the appearances of the strictest equity and justice."[9]

On statesmanship and diplomacy, Frederick reduced all moral and political practice to three principles and practices: "The first is to maintain your power, and, according to circumstances, to increase and extend it. The second is to form alliances only for your own advantage; and the third is to command fear and respect even in the most disastrous times."[10] Harsh as his maxims seem, Frederick formulated them into a doctrine of reason of state. He warned against displaying pretensions with vanity but insisted that every ruler must have "two or three eloquent men" and leave justification for his actions to them. Only when Prussia has become more powerful will she be able to assume an air of "constancy and good faith, which, at most, is fit only for the greatest powers and for petty sovereigns."[11] Of diplomats, Frederick sought "those who have the gift of expressing themselves in ambiguous terms and susceptible of a double meaning."[12] He went on to say it would not be improper for a sovereign to have political locksmiths to pick locks or open doors nor physicians to dispose of troublesome people who might be in the way. With regard to embassies, Frederick preferred envoys rather than ambassadors for it was difficult to find men of wealth and noble birth and "by adopting this system, you will save enormous sums of money every year, and, nevertheless, your affairs will be transacted all the same."[13] Yet there were cases in which embassies must be on a scale of magnificence, as when rulers sought a political or matrimonial alliance. But such instances were exceptional. Above all, neighbors must believe "that you are a dangerous monarch, who knows no other principle than that which leads to glory."[14]

It is tempting in the modern age to dismiss the insights of Thucydides and Frederick the Great or those of writers like Hobbes who spoke of a state of nature involving a "war of every man against every man" or the acute analysis of politics by Machiavelli in which might makes right. Yet diplomacy in the last two decades of the twentieth century is still conducted under the shadow of war. It is worthwhile recalling the political thought of the founding fathers. Because of man's nature and the need to remedy "the defect of better motives," the founders turned to constitutionalism as providing a system of checks and balances. They wrote of the interplay of opposite and rival interests. Because they understood the human traits of which earlier men had written, they displayed a mistrust of political power, not only that of other states but within their borders. As John Adams put it:

> Power always thinks it has a great soul and vast views
> beyond the comprehension of the weak and that it is

doing God's service when it is violating all His laws. Our passions, ambitions, love and resentment, etc., possess so much metaphysical subtlety and so much overpowering eloquence that they insinuate themselves into the understanding and the conscience and convert both to their party.

Nor was Adams alone in his concern about power. His adversary in intellectual contention during much of the period could write in 1798: "Confidence in the men of our choice . . . is . . . the parent of despotism: free government is founded in jealousy and not in confidence; it is jealousy and not confidence which prescribes limited constitutions to bind down those whom we are obliged to trust with power. . . . In questions of power then let no more be heard of confidence in man, but bind him down from mischief by the claims of the Constitution." The exercise of power and the imposing of the will of an individual or group on others was "of all known causes the greatest promoter of corruption." However the enlightenment may have shaped the thought of early Americans, their views of power reflected a sturdy realization of the hazards and reality of power. Their view of human nature was not far removed from Pascal who explained: "Man is neither angel nor brute, and the unfortunate thing is that he who would act the angel acts the brute." Whatever one's conclusions about ethics and diplomacy ultimately may be, it is important to recognize the limitations which the more sordid and selfish aspects of human nature place on the conduct of diplomacy, including diplomacy in the nuclear age.

2. THE NATURE OF DIPLOMACY AND MORALITY

The most cynical view of diplomacy is that attributed, whether rightly or not, to Sir Henry Wotton who identified "an ambassador as an honest man who is sent to lie abroad for the good of his country." The three elements which such a definition embraces are: a concept of the role of lying in diplomacy, an implication that privately the ambassador is an honest man but publicly he is something else, and an acceptance of the inevitability of the "official lie." The conventional response of moralists is to dismiss any reference to deceit as a necessary ingredient of diplomacy yet moralists run the risk of moving to an opposite extreme. As Sir Harold Nicolson wrote: "The worst kind of diplomatists are missionaries, fanatics and lawyers; the best kind are the reasonable and humane skeptics. Thus it is not religion which has been the main formative influence in diplomatic theory; it is common sense."[15] Truth telling in diplomacy is limited by the fact that diplomacy is not a system of moral philosophy. It is the application, as Sir Ernest Satow wrote, of intelligence and tact "to the conduct of official relations between independent states."[16] Honesty in diplomacy, said an experienced diplomat, doesn't mean telling everything you know.

It is of course evident that important differences exist between eighteenth or nineteenth and twentieth century diplomacy. The former involved relationships between monarchs or the members of an aristocratic elite. The latter brings together envoys of the people. In the former instance, professionals were involved while in the latter amateurs have often been engaged. Yet with all the differences, the nature of diplomacy brings into play certain common characteristics. In describing what was needed of the twentieth century diplomat, Nicolson called for "a man of experience, integrity and intelligence, a man, above all who is not swayed by emotion or prejudice, who is profoundly modest in all his dealings, who is guided only by a sense of public duty, and who understands the perils of cleverness and the virtues of reason, moderation, discretion and tact." Having said all this, Nicolson coyly added: "Mere clerks are not expected to exhibit all these difficult talents at once."[17]

The crux of the matter, as certain students of diplomacy see it, is that foreign policy is conducted by governments. As a function of their governmental responsibility it must serve the purposes of governments generally; "its primary purpose must be to preserve the union" (Lincoln) informed by the national interest and the dictates of national security. We have seen that members of a well-known group of American authorities and writers on diplomacy differ in emphasis while agreeing in their conclusions.

The champion of political realism, Hans J. Morgenthau, argued that the conduct of foreign policy is not devoid of moral significance. Political actors come under moral judgment and witness to the values of their soceieties. However, the contemporary environment of international politics is marked both by moral improvement and decline. There have been advances in respect for human life since the 15th and 16th centuries when, for example, the Republic of Venice carried on its rolls an official poisoner whose employment depended on his success in disposing of the leaders of adversary states. Compare this with the sweeping moral indignation of Winston S. Churchill described above when Stalin at Teheran proposed half mockingly but not wholly in jest that killing 50,000 officers would put an end to the threat of German aggression. Or contrast it with the public reaction in the United States to disclosures concerning possible plans for political assassinations by the CIA. The international scene in other sectors witnesses to the decline of international morality, indicating that moral restraints are weakening if not disappearing, as in distinctions in wartime between combatants and non-combatants. According to the Hague Conventions of 1899 and 1907, only soldiers ready to fight were considered combatants and objects of war, but by World War II this distinction had effectively been obliterated in the saturation bombings in which both sides engaged. The international environment, therefore, was marked by a decline in international morality brought about in part by the technology of warfare and in part by a diminution of standards concerning the sanctity of human life.

In war and peace the world has seen moral improvement in some spheres but a decline in others resulting from the fact that universal moral principles which are omnipresent are filtered through circumstances of time and place and through national concepts determining their application. The relations of universal principles to time and circumstances and to the culture and necessities of different nations and contemporary civilizations have been controlling. Particular moral imperatives are obeyed by particular nations at particular times and not by others, and this is the overarching characteristic of today's international environment.

George F. Kennan, brilliant American diplomatist and writer goes further than Professor Morgenthau in writing:

The governing of human beings is not a moral exercise. It is a practical function made necessary, regrettably, by the need for order in social relationships and for a collective discipline to control the behavior of that large majority of mankind who are too weak and selfish to control their own behavior useful on the basis of individual judgment and conscience.[18]

Ambassador Kennan declares further that "government, particularly democratic government, is an agent and not a principal." No more than any other agent (for example, the corporation or the church, especially since the Protestant Reformation) can it substitute itself for the conscience of the principal. In a particularly strongly worded statement applying this thought to the American government as agent of the American people, Mr. Kennan asserts:

The government could undertake to express and to implement the moral impulses of so great a mass of people only if there were a high degree of consensus among them on such question as: what is good and what is bad? and to what extent is it the duty of American society to make moral judgments on behalf of others and to improve them from the standpoint of those judgments? Such consensus would be difficult to achieve even if we were dealing with a highly homogeneous population, with firm and unanimously-accepted concepts of an ethical nature as well as of the duties and powers of the state. In the case of a polyglot assemblage of people such as our own, it would be quite impossible. If our government should set out to pursue moral purposes in foreign policy, on what would it base itself? Whose outlooks, philosophy, religious concepts would it choose to express? Imbedded in our population are hundreds of different traditions, beliefs, assumptions and reactions in this field. Are we to assume that it, the government, knows what is right and wrong, has imparted this knowledge to the people at large, and obtained their mandate to proceed to bring about the triumph of what is right, on a worldwide scale?

Opposed to the views of diplomatic writers is a large and respected body of thought resulting from international law writings. The former American Judge on the International Court of Justice, Philip Jessup, has singled out five criteria as essential to an ethical and therefore a successful foreign policy: sincerity, loyalty, legality, humanitarianism" and what he has called "proper objectives." By sincerity he means the same as honesty or an absence of deceit, vital as he sees it, especially in peacetime. A government suffers from such labels as that it is not to be trusted. Judge Jessup acknowledges there may be imperatives which lead to deceit of a government's own citizenry but these must find justification if at all under "proper objectives." Louis Halle who belongs to the first group of diplomatic writers offers a dissenting commentary on this point saying:

> From 1955 to 1960 . . . the United States regularly sent its U-2 spy planes over the Soviet Union at high altitudes to locate military installations and report on military activities. Presumably, such planes would have been able to detect any preparations for a surprise attack on the United States in time to give warning . . . A Soviet system of espionage operating inside the United States was alert to detect any preparations for a surprise attack on the Soviet Union. This mutual espionage contributed to the preservation of the peace, because the observations of the spies on either side, showing that the other was not preparing a surprise attack, enabled each to remain calm and restrained. If such observations had not been available, each side might have been the victim of panic—making rumors that would have impelled it to feel that its survival depended on striking before the other was able to realize some rumored intention of doing so itself.

Halle goes on:

> However, in 1960 when an American U-2, illegally violating another country's air space, was shot down in the middle of the Soviet Union, many idealists in the West were shocked to learn that such espionage by the United States had been going on, for they regarded it as both immoral and incompatible with the advancement of the cause of peace.

> Peace is more secure today, and the prospects of arms control are better, to the extent that the Soviet Union and the United States, through their espionage (in which satellites have replaced spy planes), can each be sure of what armaments the other possesses.

There are significant differences between diplomatic analysts and international lawyers, therefore, on truth-telling. The former are more inclined to say that while there is a universal moral code of truth-telling, there are differing social contexts in which it is applied. In personal and national affairs, men operate within an integrated society where lying is seldom necessary. Mayor Daley's creed for Chicago politics was that a politician's last resource is his word and that lying is not good politics ("if you must lie, it is better not to say anything.") International affairs differ and the difference is one between conditions of civilization and conditions of nature, where because of the half anarchic character of international society "one man is to another as a wolf." However, for the second group of writers, the international lawyers, truth-telling is an aspect of sincerity plus loyalty plus legality. Law's basic norm—*Pacta sunt servanda*—is a part not only of our own moral creed but of the Koran and other religious teachings. Pragmatism and morality came together in the Hague and the Geneva Conventions on the treatment of civilians and prisoners evolving from the pragmatic test of reciprocity. Judge Jessup states:

> the principle or rule that a treaty secured by the application of force or threats to the person of the negotiator is void, is an illustration of a moral base for a legal rule. The bombing of Cambodia by the Nixon administration is an example of illegal, immoral and bad policy. The Mayaguez affair is another similar example as it was also deceitful in its alleged justification.

Judge Hardy Dillard, former American judge on the International Court of Justice and Virginia Law School Dean went further. International law, for him, was not a legal straitjacket or an abstract and inflexible set of rules. It could be made to serve the security interests of the United States. Its putative advantages in specific policy choices could be measured against its costs. For him, the U-2 flight was a mistaken act because its alleged advantages were outweighed by its costs. Law has a constitutive function by ordering the bully to do what is right. It is designed not to settle but to absorb disputes. Today the world is governed by a network of international treaties. Some 760 fat volumes of U.N. Treaties, designed to regulate international life, have been registered since World War II by the U.N. Secretariat. Nations are free to invoke or not this body of law, but it is a factor to be taken into account as a guide to policy decision.

It is fallacious to say law is obligatory and policy voluntary. *Pacta sunt servanda* for Judge Dillard didn't mean that all treaties have to be observed all the time. The ultimate value of Article 2, Paragraph 4, of the U.N. Charter on the use or threat of force against the territorial integrity of sovereign states or of international treaties regarding human rights was that certain moral and political positions are now in place, policies have been forged into solemn agreements, and important matters are no longer solely a matter of domestic jurisdiction. To paraphrase Justice Holmes, taking law into account is not a duty but only a necessity; the end products or results of diplomacy can't be ignored. Moralistic finger shaking may prove more an irritant than a solution but in every policy decision the good of invoking the law must be weighed against its disadvantages. All history is a tension between heritage and heresy; law and policy must mediate conflicting demands for stability and change. Taking a moral stand is different from moralizing about it.

3. PRACTICAL MORALITY AND DIPLOMACY

The prevailing approach to the ethical dimension of diplomacy is one which has placed stress on morality pure and simple. Oftentimes defenders of this approach have been driven to take positions their critics have described as moralism and legalism. Those who question whether morality exists for diplomacy ask whether there exist more proximate moral positions that can be discussed under the heading practical morality.

One such approach is that of workability as opposed to the proclamation of abstract moral principles. Diplomatists put the stress on workability: the objective of foreign policy should be as closely related to the reduction of human suffering and contribution to the welfare of people as possible, not the unqualified triumph of abstract principle. Moral appeals to the generality of mankind or the mass of the people too often constitute not morality but Pharisaism.

Whatever the short-run advantages of this approach, it has floundered in the long run because an individual or a nation who claims an achieved morality that others have a duty to follow does so on an assumption of having itself attained moral perfection. Manichaeanism is a false religion which sees the world as divided between good guys and bad guys and this disease has infected American thinking on foreign policy. Since World War I, we have divided the world into peace-loving and aggressor, freedom-loving and communist states and based foreign policy on such a distinction. The road to Vietnam lies not in the nefarious acts of the "best and the brightest" but upon indiscriminate anti-communist thinking which ignores the test of workability. The almost inevitable result of Manichaeanism is a moral crusade, war or the threat of war and genocide (it is worth remembering that certain allied leaders who fought a war against Hitler who exterminated millions of Jews saw the "solution" to the German problem in the extermination, in turn, of thousands of Germans).

Workability is also the test of certain diplomatic historians, notable among them being the cold war historian, Norman Graebner of the University of Virginia. History suggests that whenever the United States has introduced towering humanitarian objectives as the guide to policy it has often added to rather than diminished human suffering and subsequently abandoned such unworkable policies. In our time, Secretary Dulles' liberation foreign policy, offered by the Republicans as a more dynamic alternative to the postwar policy of containment, inspired Hungarian freedom fighters to revolt only then to discover that American national interest and the facts of geography and power precluded American intervention.

For the first thirty years of our history, the guiding principle was that the new nation through its moral and political example offered a beacon light for the rest of the world. Spokesmen for two approaches contended with one another. Benjamin Franklin exemplified one approach when he wrote: "Establishing the liberties of America will not only make the people happy, but will have some effect in diminishing the misery of those, who in other parts of the world groan under despotism." Thereafter every major European revolution against monarchy and aristocracy evoked popular demands that the United States underwrite its cause and thereby that of humanity. Graebner observes, however, that "never were the repeated references to the American mission in the nineteenth century the actual determinants of policy." These demands collided with an even stronger American tradition that the nation concern itself with those finite goals which served the national interest. Alexander Hamilton warned in his "Pacificus" and "Americanus" letters that the only sure guide was the national interest. George Washington resisted the popular mass movement lead by Citizen Genet for intervention on the side of the French Revolution on grounds that "no nation is to be trusted further than it is bound by its interest; and no prudent statesman or politician will venture to depart from it." Even American idealists such as Thomas Jefferson, James Madison, Henry Clay, and Abraham Lincoln, especially when they were responsible for decision-making, were less concerned with American involvement in revolutions abroad than in building a good society and preserving national security. When President James K. Polk in 1845 sought to universalize the American interest in the Western Hemisphere under the Monroe Doctrine, John C. Calhoun argued in the Senate that the ends of policy had to be calculated by the means available. It was, he maintained:

> the part of wisdom to elect wise ends in a wise manner. No wise man, with a full understanding of the subject, could pledge himself, by declaration, to do that which was beyond the power of execution, and without mature reflection as to the consequences. There would be no dignity in it. True dignity consists in making no declaration which we are not prepared to maintain. If we make the declaration, we ought to be prepared to carry it into effect against all opposition.

Professor Graebner argues that a shift in the American approach to foreign policy occurred with President Woodrow Wilson, foreshadowed by President William McKinley's defense of the Spanish American War and the acquisition of the Philippines based on sentiment rather than clearly defined national interests. "None of the nineteenth century revolutions in Europe or Asia succeeded or failed because of what the United States did or did not do. They reflected the worldwide trend toward self-determination and democratic forms of government, supported by American model, nothing more." With Wilson, idealism and sometimes moralism replaced political realism as the cornerstone of a new world order. Maintenance of the status quo was identified with universal democracy and the Versailles peace structure; Americans linked that status quo with the abstract moral and legal principles of the League of Nations rather than a body of clearly defined interests to be defended through diplomacy and war. The goals of a universal moral order were in tension with the policies of nations who could not see their interests as served by strict observance of that order. The Japanese and the Germans turned to war in part because their leaders were able to rally their publics against the real and imagined injustice of the status quo and in part because the principles of peaceful change did not satisfy the interests of all nations equally (the British, French, Belgian, Dutch and even American Empires were left untouched by the peace settlement but not those of Germany, Austria and Japan). Professor Graebner writes: "In its relations with Japan the United States sought peace. But its proposals [fueled by the moral indignation of leaders such as Cordell Hull], based on the assumption that the right belonged totally to the status quo sought not compromise but capitulation. The capitulation never came." History repeated itself in some respects following World War II. American efforts to apply the doctrine of self-determination failed to undo specific repressions which existed behind the Iron and Bamboo curtains. Graebner concludes:

> The Wilsonian appeal ... could not prevent the destruction of the Versailles order; the postwar appeal to the Atlantic Charter could not restore it ... What the American experience, in many ways unique, has demonstrated is the fact that policy goals unsupported by generally recognizable interests will not receive much credence elsewhere.[19]

There is no dignity in goals a nation is not prepared to carry into effect measured by all possible consequences.

The international law school's response to the diplomatists' critique is to question whether words and solemn commitments do not have an effect in and of themselves. Important ideas enshrined in the American Declaration of Independence have been written into solemn international treaties; for example, the Declaration and Covenants of Human Rights. (The diplomatists asked whether failure to ratify the Covenants gave America a strong platform from which to speak.) Words and ideas have consequences and the evidence there is something universal about human rights and

fundamental freedoms is attested in the vocabulary even of the communist and totalitarian states. (Niebuhr once wrote that "Hypocrisy
is the tribute that vice pays to virtue.") A nation acts by speaking
out for its values and there are costs in remaining silent. (Judge
Dillard introduces the qualification that in international law protest indicated nonacquiescence, but failure to protest does *not*
indicate acquiescence.)

Policy-makers ask if it is not legitimate to include in the national
interest principles intended to arouse public support and enthusiasm for a given foreign policy. It was argued in the late 1970s that
because of President Carter's human rights policies the world
came to believe again in the American vision, testimony to the
power of words and ideas. In the days of the founding fathers, the
United States was powerless to work its will; now it has become the
most powerful nation in the world, its words more surely attended
to. (Some see in this fact new responsibilities; whereas others warn
against the corruption of power. Perhaps Niebuhr's counsel helps
reconcile these differences: "Nations, as individuals, may be assailed
by contradictory temptations. They may be tempted to flee the
responsibilities of their power or refuse to develop their potentialities. But they may also refuse to recognize the limits of their
possibilities and seek greater power than is given to mortals.")

For the international lawyer, the national interest is too narrow
a concept. Enforcement is misconceived if keyed exclusively to
physical enforcement. (The statement, "the Supreme Court has
spoken, now let it enforce its decision" must be weighed against
the success of the courts, say, in requiring President Nixon to give
up the tapes despite the powers of the President as Commander in
Chief.) There is only one example in the fifty year history of the
World Court of a nation refusing to abide by a judgment, Albania
in the Corfu Channel case. Judge Lauterpacht wrote that the
French Declaration of Human Rights was more powerful than all
the battalions of Napoleon. Judge Dillard recognized the futility of
nations proposing things that couldn't be done effectively and
raising false expectations (example, rolling back the Iron Curtain).
He quoted Lord Balfour on the need for restraint in making griev-
ances public. However, he insisted it was too narrow in approach
to say nations can't do anything unless they can enforce it; there
are other forms of pressures. Law may not command but it can
affect what nations do in justifying their actions. If moral state-

ments and standards are irrelevant, why do nations bother to justify themselves as measured by those standards. There are signs that even the Russians respond and are sensitive to moral appeals.

Whether other nations are sensitive or not, the question remains whether proclaiming moral principles does more harm than good. Workability and attention to consequences leads diplomatists to measure developments that are likely or possible in the future. It will not do to settle the issues involved by saying the United States has again given the world a vision of hope. The question involving practical morality is where will that vision lead and will the overall effects be better or worse than what has gone before.

If the first issue between the diplomatic analysts and historians and the international lawyer is workability, the second is the nature of the international society. The diplomatic school sees the world of American foreign policy as subject to many of the same rules and constraints known at the founding of the republic. To the question posed by the historian Carl Becker at the end of World War II, *How New Will the Better World Be,* they answered it is neither wholly new nor necessarily better. Why? Because of the nature of man, of international politics and the persistence of the nation state system. Professor Morgenthau stated:

> the purpose of foreign policy is not to bring enlightment or happiness to the rest of the world but to take care of the life, liberty and happiness of the American people.

At the same time, Morgenthau acknowledged that national interest in contemporary American foreign policy must be defined in terms which transcend 19th century concepts of national interest. In a certain sense, all nation states, large and small, are obsolete; they no longer adequately meet human needs within national boundaries. Man's protection of the environment and preservation and distribution of natural resources require the cooperative efforts of communities of sovereign states. Yet, however obsolete the present international system may be, national leaders are still held responsible for the wise conduct of their nation's foreign policy, thus maintaining the requirements of historic international politics until the day when a new international system may come into being.

International lawyers are more inclined to argue the existence of a new and better world, the birth of an embryonic world community. The Charter of the United Nations and the Declaration and some nineteen Covenants of Human Rights are said to embody core principles of human rights and fundamental freedoms foreshadowed in the American Declaration of Independence. To defend human rights abroad, therefore, is not to act in contravention of Article 2, Paragraph 7—the domestic jurisdiction clause of the United Nations. Judge Philip C. Jessup quoted Secretary of State Elihu Root writing in 1906 to the American Ambassador in St. Petersburg regarding a protest concerning the persecution of Jews in Russia:

> I think it may do some good, though I do not feel sure of it. I do not know how it will be received. It may merely give offense. I am sure that to go further would do harm. I am sure also that to publish here the fact that such a dispatch has been sent would do harm, and serious harm to the unfortunate people whom we desire to help. Any possible good effect must be looked for in absolutely confidential communication to the Russian Government. The publication that any communication has been made would inevitably tend to prevent the Russian government from acting, to increase the anti-Jewish feelings and to make further massacres more probable.

But then Judge Jessup added that the situation today may differ "since human rights have become the subject of international agreements."

Each of the great political traditions has its own conception of human values and the good life. For the Christian belief in God and serving one's fellow man is uppermost in the Christian hierarchy of values. For the disciple of classical political thought the search for virtue in society is the highest calling. For modern political thinkers, the establishment of the best social and constitutional arrangements within existing societies is the foremost objective. The Christian and the classical traditions depend on certain objective values and standards within society and the political process. The values of the two older traditions are ultimately transcendent while those of modern political thought are immanent. Contemporary exceptions include those political theories for which the earlier traditions have residual importance, such as those of the founding fathers of the American constitutional and political system.

The prospects of all three political traditions have been diminished, however, by certain forces at work within the present-day nation-state. Christian thought from its beginnings assumed that man necessarily and inevitably lived in two worlds, the city of man and the city of God. The former was the temporary realm of contingencies, imperfection, and sin; the latter was the enduring realm of certainty, perfection, and the good. The one was realizable here and now, the other in eternity. The social and political order was structured to reflect, partially at least, the reality of the two worlds. The Christian vision provided for both a horizontal and vertical dimension in human life, with men reaching out to one another in the social order and seeking to know God in the spiritual order. Government was the custodian of the social and political order and citizens were enjoined to give to Caesar what was Caesar's. The church was the custodian of the spiritual order and believers were enjoined to serve God with what was God's.

The rise of the modern nation-state and the breakdown of the Corpus Christianum diminished, if it did not destroy, the vision of the two cities. The authority of the one universal church was undermined by the Reformation and the Renaissance. The religion of the prince within emerging political societies determined the religion of the people. Religion and patriotism tended to reenforce one another whereas they had earlier constituted a system of checks and balances interacting with one another. If the universal Catholic Church was in part responsible for the union of the two because of its tendency to equate and make itself coextensive with the city of God, the embryonic nation-state was also responsible by becoming the repository of individual and group morality in order to assure political cohesion. Whereas the church had taught believers the commandment "Thou shalt not kill," princes and rulers taught "Thou shalt kill to preserve the nation-state."

Moreover, other forces were at work weakening the hold of the Christian tradition. The Christian tradition in its historical formulation presupposed a world of sheep and shepherd. The modern era has witnessed the growth of ever more complex societies in which the individual to whom Christianity ministered was further and further removed from primary human relations with his fellow men. The great society supplanted the good Samaritan. Furthermore, Christianity itself became more and more fragmented. In America a great Civil War found men praying to the same God and justifying their acts from the same Scriptures. During the conflict President Abraham Lincoln wrote that "each party claims to act in accordance with the will of God. Both *may* be, and one *must* be wrong. God can not be *for,* and *against* the same thing at the same time." In recent days Martin Luther King and Jerry Falwell invoked the Scriptures to defend actions affecting millions of people in diametrically opposite ways. Maintaining a universal Christian tradition is complicated by the rise of sovereign nation-states. The nation fills the minds and hearts of men everywhere with particular experiences and with particular concepts of political philosophy, particular standards of political morality, and particular goals of political action, to paraphrase Morgenthau.

If the Christian tradition has been challenged by the circumstances surrounding the modern nation-state, the classical tradition was threatened in a similar way. Modernity has brought about a shift, it is argued, from discussions of the good man and the good state to discourse on political power and political tactics. Classical political philosophy was not unaware of the realities of good and evil in human nature. The Platonic dialogues are filled with examples of cynical and selfish men overriding reason and virtue in their political attitudes and conduct. Yet for the philosopher, contemplating the human drama as a whole, reason was superior to the irrational and virtue was the standard by which cynicism and selfishness were judged. Man approached his true and best nature in participating in the social and political order. He realized himself as a social animal.

Classicists maintained, however, that man's fulfillment was most attainable within the polity, a small-sized political community in which face-to-face political discourse occurred. By contrast, the citizen in the larger nation-states has little, if any, contact with his rulers. He is remote from the scene of urgent problems and unable to comprehend the complex issues on which he must decide. The closest aide to President Lyndon B. Johnson observed that nuclear questions escaped him no matter how faithfully he studied them. Jack Valenti was forced to find scientists he could trust. Comprehension required scientific and technical knowledge which only scientific specialists possessed.

The history of modern times throws a cloud over the case that classicists make for reason and virtue. Wise students of political history such as Reinhold Niebuhr, Herbert Butterfield, and Hans J.

Morgenthau have traced the influence of the irrational in politics. The German people, whose culture matched any in Europe, followed a fanatical leader, Hitler, who stirred popular emotions with slogans depicting the Germans as racially superior. Legislative assemblies, intended for prudent deliberation, become the scene of chauvinist and bellicose debate. National self-determination, which had promised satisfaction and peace to the world's people, was successfully invoked by Hitler for the annexation of the Sudetenland. Reason proved defective in anticipating the consequences of thousands of apparently reasonable acts. Unintended and unforeseen consequences of reasonable historical acts outweighed the expected or intended results. Thus the Protestant Reformation rested on the proposition that individuals should be free to read and interpret the Bible, but by strengthening nationalism, it caused a weakening of individualism. The French Revolution, which promised liberty, equality, and fraternity, led to the submergence of liberty and equality in the Napoleonic Empire.

To recite a litany of individual virtues when individuals are swallowed up in big government, big labor, or big management seems less relevant in the modern world. More germane are discussions of the problems of hard-pressed individuals seeking to reconcile competing virtues. The busy executive, for whom long hours and neglect of family are sometimes required to assure profits and livelihood, struggles to be a good father. For the devoted parent caring for children may necessitate overlooking his own parents. Being a man of virtue and principle may not be enough under these circumstances. The truly virtuous man has to find his way through a maze of conflicting principles.

If Christian and classical thought are criticized for too much opposition to modernity and too great a faith in historical political values, modern political thought links modernity with progress. Whereas the older traditions stand in opposition to present trends, modern political theory tends to sanctify them. It glorifies the state and, more particularly, certain branches of government which it favors, one after the other, as the cycle turns. Transposed to the international scene, modern thought manifests an exaggerated confidence in institutions as instruments for transforming international politics. The rise and fall of popular enthusiasm for each of these institutions in turn has thrown into question the judgment of modern thought. It has also led some contemporary thinkers to reopen the question of the relevance of Christian and classical thought to present-day problems.

Not only has the rise of the nation-state profoundly affected the relation of the great political traditions to politics but so have the changing patterns of international politics and diplomacy. Historically, the Christian and classical political traditions assumed a consensus on values within the Christian and classical worlds. Four developments have altered the political world within which any of the historic traditions must operate. First, a worldwide system of political ideologies and conflicting religious faiths has replaced the Christian Europe of which historians like Christopher Dawson wrote in tracing the formation of Western Christendom. Universal Christendom lost out to a pluralistic international system of competing nation-states and cultures. Second, the political faiths which inspired men took on the characteristics of the terrestial world rather than the adornments of the heavenly city. To the extent the latter existed at all it was a "this worldly" utopia. Carl Becker described the heavenly city of the eighteenth-century philosophers; Marx and Lenin elaborated a creed that identified the end of history with the Marxist classless society. Salvation was achievable here and now and its standards were not outside, but within, history. The direct application to international problems of the Christian tradition was undermined by the breakdown of a consensus on values and the disappearance of faith in effective objective moral principles outside history.

Two other developments coincided with and reenforced the above mentioned changes. They profoundly affected the relevance of the classical tradition. One of these was a consequence of the vast increase in the size of viable political units. The movement from city-states to nation-states culminated in the postwar emergence of the superpowers. That good men would create good regimes became a difficult proposition to sustain. Good and bad men alike seized power in large collective states claiming that only they were capable of solving the momentous social problems of great masses of people. Events that good men had prophesied were rationally impossible, such as global depressions, world wars, and totalitarianism, followed one another in rapid succession. Large populations responded to programs whose defenders argued that they served all the people. If Americans had any doubt concerning the far-reaching effects of this third development, they had only to compare the deliberative processes of leaders addressing the New England town meeting with Mussolini or Hitler haranguing the German and Italian people with the claim, "forty million Italians (Germans) can't be wrong." In short, the concept of popular sovereignty replaced that of personal virtue.

A fourth development was the radical transformation of political communication. Classical political thought had maintained that personal and collective morality were indivisible. In the modern era not only totalitarian rulers but democratic leaders determined what was moral and right in terms of the interests of states. While certain moral principles applicable to individuals survived in the eighteenth-century idea of raison d'etat, as Machiavelli had clung to the concept of virtue, contemporary rulers maintained that whatever their personal moral standards on war or slavery, national unity and preserving the state took precedence and were controlling. Thus both Christian and classical thought lost a large measure of their force in the face of far-reaching historical changes.

Modern political thought appeared to offer an alternative to the decline of the ancient traditions. Especially liberalism held out the promise to the great mass of the people of human improvement through universal public education. Today's pressing problems would yield to the workings of free society. Individuals, ever more enlightened by science and reason, would throw off human traits and archaic political ideas and institutions that had led throughout history to conflict and war. Individual man pursuing his selfish interests would be guided nationally and internationally as if by a hidden hand to act for the common good. Nationally the process would operate in free-market economies guaranteed to serve the general welfare. ("What is good for General Motors is good for America," a cabinet member in the Eisenhower administration prophesied.) Internationally, Woodrow Wilson proclaimed that national self-determination would lead to a peaceful world, never dreaming that Hitler would invoke a Wilsonian principle to justify his expansionist policies. Moreover, national and international economic stagnation in the 1930s led millions of people to turn to new and more dynamic collectivist solutions.

Not only did the four developments sound the death knell for the effectiveness and coherence of the three great political traditions; another factor sped the disintegration of the international political order. The values which had introduced a limited degree of stability within single political communities proved ineffective on the international stage. The standards that had assured relative peace within nations proved ineffectual or largely irrelevant in international affairs. What was disallowed or dealt with as an exception to the normal processes of national societies was accepted as inevitable in international society. While civil war represented the breakdown of the political order within nations, war was accepted as the continuation of diplomacy by other means in relations among nation-states.

The problem, as Reinhold Niebuhr discussed it in a succession of treatises on foreign policy, was that in international politics no single moral principle existed for ordering all other separate moral principles. In international politics, rough-and-ready norms such as "damage limitation" became the overarching principles rather than such benign standards as the quest for the good society or for communities aimed at human self-fulfillment. In the end modern political thought which had promised a new and better world became an even more tragic victim to history than Christian or classical thought.

For these reasons the culmination of history on the international stage was not the heavenly city but the nuclear age. The end of warfare which liberal political thinkers had predicted yielded to the specter of warfare as universal human destruction. Ironically, human advancement and progress led not to refutation of ancient political truths but to their rediscovery. Prudence has once more become the master virtue in international politics at a moment in time when anything less is a threat to human existence. But political prudence was an idea that Aristotle set forth as a guide for political practice as distinct from political contemplation. From Aristotle and Augustine through Edmund Burke to Niebuhr and John Courtney Murray, prudence as an operative political principle was kept alive not as rigid formulation or precise definition of what was right or wrong but as the concept of practical reason may dictate under a given set of circumstances. Practical morality involves the reconciliation of what is morally desirable and politically possible. It offers at most a few absolutes but many practical possibilities. Prudence is the central precept in the ancient tradition of moral reasoning. It recognizes the need for the moral man in an immoral world to find his way through "a maze of conflicting moral principles" no one of which reigns supreme.

Thus justice is a moral objective in international politics but so is international peace. Freedom is a value which must compete with national security. In the same way that the Supreme Court within the United States declared that freedom doesn't give men the right to cry fire in a crowded theater, so internationally the establishment of free states everywhere cannot justify overriding the necessity for order or survival in the newer and poorer nation-states. Resistance to the spread of communism, which is a clear objective of Americans, may clash with the realities of communist societies that are unlikely to change except through the historic process. Nations like China and Yugoslavia work their way through to their own "best possible regimes." Indiscriminate anticommunism can no more be equated with political prudence as a coherent foreign policy for Americans than indiscriminate world revolution can for the Soviet Union.

National interest as a guide to diplomacy may at first glance seem remote from the ancient ideas of prudence of Christian and classical writers. Yet what political realism and practical reason have in common is acceptance of the best solution appropriate to particular circumstances. Philosophers and reformers may offer more glittering answers to the world's problems, but it is unlikely any other approach can come closer to a practical way of thinking. Every foreign policy decision presently has its military, political, and Soviet-American dimension. Too often policymakers choose policies that apply exclusively to one or the other dimension. Prudence requires attention to all three dimensions and an attempt to find the best possible solutions after giving weight to all three. Tragically, the political process by which men come to office in the United States is unlikely to elect men with the capacity to think clearly in all three dimensions at once. Yet anything less will likely lead to disaster in American diplomacy.

4. SOME MODEST CONCLUSIONS ABOUT MORALITY AND DIPLOMACY

If morality is assumed to involve the early attainment of a set of towering and novel moral principles transforming the world then the cynics are right that there is no ethical dimension to diplomacy. However if such goals as workability, damage limitation and practical morality are accepted as worthy of the name morality, an opposite conclusion is possible. The moral content of diplomacy is both more modest and important than critics would suggest. The harmonizing of sometimes conflicting but possibly convergent national interests is a moral and political process. Drawing the poison out of a conflict as if by a poultice is an important moral aim. Framing an agreement through long and arduous diplomatic negotiations is a pursuit of enduring value, whether the end product is a formal legal treaty or a tacit agreement. Discovering an exit from war and the end to military conflict through truce negotiations is an essentially moral process. Settling a boundary dispute, limiting an arms race, bringing about the relaxation of tensions or arranging cultural exchanges or trade relations are all worthy purposes.

If one asks what is common to the quest for each of the moral purposes enumerated above it is that they can be pursued only through some form or another of diplomatic processes. Sometimes hard bargaining will be required, other times long and protracted negotiations. Whatever the form of the search for these moral ends, the diplomatic process is vital to their attainment. Avoidance of Soviet occupation of Poland has such primacy that the Pope and the military ruler of Poland may have "cut a deal" that more militant groups would oppose. The diplomatic process may serve higher ends while the means appear morally ambiguous. In recognizing this fact, we have moved much closer to a fuller perception of the ethical dimension of diplomacy.

NOTES

1. June Bingham, *Courage to Change: An Introduction to the Life and Thought of Reinhold Niebuhr,* New York: Charles Scribner's Sons, 1961, 62.
2. Quoted in A. C. F. Beales, a Short History of English Liberalism, 195.
3. *House of Commons Debates,* Fifth Series, 1946, Vol. 419, 1262.
4. Frederick the Great, *Origin of the Bismarck Policy,* European Pamphlets, Vol. 12, Boston: Crosby, Damrell, 100 Washington Street, 1870, 6.
5. *Ibid.,* 12.
6. *Ibid.,* 21.

7. *Ibid.,* 22.
8. *Ibid.*
9. *Ibid.,* 23.
10. *Ibid.,* 43.
11. *Ibid.,* 48.
12. *Ibid.,* 48–49.
13. *Ibid.,* 50.
14. *Ibid.,* 51.
15. Sir Harold Nicolson, *Diplomacy,* London: Oxford University Press, 1939, 50.
16. Quoted in *Ibid.,* 45–46.
17. *Ibid.,* 76.
18. Quotations from Morgenthau, Kennan, Halle and Jessup are taken from unpublished papers written for a conference on "Morality and Foreign Policy" held in Charlottesville, Virginia in June, 1977, and jointly sponsored by the Department of State and the University of Virginia.
19. Presentation at the Virginia Conference.

PART TWO

Statesmen
And Problems

Human Rights and
National Sovereignty

Few problems in contemporary international relations illustrate more graphically the interplay between moralism, cynicism, and morality. Successive administrations have moved to one or the other extreme in formulating human rights policies. Critics charged the Carter administration with exaggerating the prospects of human rights in countries around the world. In his campaign for promoting publicly the achievement of human rights everywhere despite the absence in some cultures and regions of the underlying moral foundations, Carter's approach was called moralistic. Following Carter, the Reagan administration was critized for a rather cynical view of the character of regimes such as the military government of Argentina.

Going further, some critics maintain that the human rights policies of the Carter administration ignored the sovereignty of nation states whose domestic affairs were not properly the concern of other sovereign states. Even the Charter of the United Nations in the famous domestic jurisdiction clause of Article 2, Paragraph 7, recognizes sovereignty. Theorists of international politics speak of the impenetrability of nation states. Sovereignty assumes the right of constitutionally responsible authorities to make decisions on matters within a nation's domestic jurisdiction. The Carter administration may have misjudged the force of sovereignty.

On the other hand, those who question the policies of the Reagan administration insist that it has failed to appreciate the network of relations which bind nation states together in an interdependent world. In refusing to recognize the authority of the International Court on U.S. activities in Central America for two years on issues arising, for example, from the CIA mining without

warning of Nicaraguan harbors, the administration ignored international law which for some issues stands above national sovereignty.

1. REASON OF STATE

On the issue of political authority in another era, the debate over
what the French call *raison d'etat* or "reason of state" illustrates the
tension between the general and the particular. Sir Herbert Butterfield, former Vice Chancellor of Cambridge University and founding
Chairman of the British Committee on the Theory of International
Relations discussed this concept in the first Martin Wight Memorial Lecture delivered at the University of Sussex on April 23, 1975.
Using the subtitle "The Relations Between Morality and Government," Butterfield points out that the idea of reason of state has
become almost a fossil or an archaism in the twentieth century. Yet
in the early seventeenth century, it found its way into discussions in
the marketplace of international diplomacy. Cardinal Richelieu in
his *Political Testament* spoke of reason "as the rule of conduct for
a state." Different writers spoke of "national reason" or "civil
reasoning" as appropriate not alone to politics and government
but, as variously interpreted, the fundamental principle of governance for the state.

The concept of the state, Butterfield observes, goes back to the
Latin "status" meaning in the ancient world something approaching
"condition" or "standing." Professor F. M. Powicke in his Presidential Address appearing in "Transactions of the Royal Historical
Society," 4th series, vol. XIX, p. 9, "interpreted the classical Latin
term as "that which gives validity to a thing." The Italian equivalent,
"stato," we are told, occurs more than a hundred times in Machiavelli's *Prince* without carrying the ethical implications of the Greek
polis or the Latin *republica*. From 1600, the idea of the state was to
expand in its meaning beyond the concept of "a power apparatus"
associated with Machiavelli. Ambiguity and inconsistency surrounded the term, however, which sometimes referred only to the
art of government and other times referred to the founding, maintenance and expansion of the state. At times, "reason of state" meant
statecraft and at other times it appeared to be used to override
ordinary reason. Certain Catholic writers distinguished between
"good" reason of state but others used the idea to convey "the logic

of state interests." Some publicists saw the concept as a universal one while others suggested that every one of the different kinds of states had its own version of "raison d'etat." Richelieu not only argued that this principle was the ruling force undergirding all state activity but introduced a religious view of the nature and purpose of the state.

At the end of the sixteenth century, the teachings of Machiavelli had gained a hold on statesmen and writers and for many of them politics was associated with power politics, however offensive this idea may have been then and now. The idea of necessity was also imported into discussions of politics justifying the right and duty of the king and his associates to override positive law in the service of well-recognized common interests. For the prince or the man conspiring to be the prince, certain harsh maxims are introduced by Machiavelli not as maxims of righteous conduct but as rules to be followed by the ruler if he wished to be successful in politics.

The concept of "reason of state" achieved a more complete expression in seventeenth century France particularly in the writings and actions of Richelieu and Louis XIV. France in 1600 suffered from the fragmentation of political authority. "Authority had been splintered into a jig-saw puzzle of local autonomies, special privileged areas, all of which were the characteristics of the *ancien regime* and had been vastly increased during recent decades of civil war. Across the entire map there was a vast thick forest of prescriptive rights—peculiar prerogatives attached now to certain individuals, now to certain towns, now to certain landed property, now to certain public offices, now to social groups, now to institutions. Confronted by this host of privileges and immunities the central government during the course of centuries would hardly be able to hold its own, until, from 1789, the remnants of them became the main target of the French Revolution." (Sir Herbert Butterfield, *Raison D'Etat,* Sussex, England: University of Sussex, 1975, p. 13).

Against this state of affairs, Richelieu argued that the subjects of the regime, including princes of the royal family who might rebel, must be made subordinate to the public power. Government officials, privileged corporations of town and countryside and even the King were subordinate to the idea of state. In foreign policy too, especially in the eighteenth century, the monarch was guided by the interest of state, the general welfare and public safety rather than by the primacy of dynastic ambitions or family objectives. It is said that Richelieu's major purpose was state-building and Meinecke observed that without the commanding force of the idea of state, millions of overmighty subjects would have become centers of self-regarding authority. Political unification rested on the idea of the state and with all the controversy, human suffering and threats to divine law or natural morality which most writers agreed ought not to be overridden, the main task of statesmanship was to create and preserve viable political units. The powers of the state were those which were essential in the last resort expanded to assure survival especially in emergencies but also intended to serve the general welfare and the broad interests of the body politics. Imbedded in Richelieu's *Political Testament* were guides to the political relations among states such as the idea of continuous negotiations even when countries go to war. And although he held that the individual Christian should forgive the person who injured him, he held that failure to punish attacks on the body politic represented the most fatal kind of weakness in government. He reproached Louis XIII for failure to put down conspiracies and rebellions and quoted Christian theologians to justify the punishment of threats to and offences against the state. Governments must act while they still have the capacity to act and their actions must be prompt and decisive. Preventive imprisonment may in some cases be a more humane alternative than execution. The underlying justification for stern acts by the state depends on the idea of "reason of state" equated with the common good or public safety.

The idea of "*raison d'etat*" has a quaint if not archaic meaning in the twentieth century and yet it remains as the historical antecedent of much of present day political discussion. One starting point in the discussion of the tension between universal human rights and national sovereignty is a recognition that the sovereign nation state has evolved to serve broader interests. It is fashionable in the 1980s to write of the obsolescence of the nation state which for the industrial or developed countries no longer is sufficient to assure either national security or the general social and economic welfare. Yet the situation in the developing countries especially remains not wholly dissimilar from that described in *Political Testament*. Tribal loyalties, separatist groups and local power centers threaten political unification; fragmentary loyalties and interests are more likely to be transcended by the nation than by worldwide authorities. The highest form of unity for the non-industrial world may be national unity. Moreover, the risks of political devolution are not confined to the developing world as evidenced in Canada, Ireland and even the United Kingdom. The Soviet Union is opposed to expanded rights for minorities and in particular the Jews because the independence of one group is viewed as a threat by others to the survival of the present political regime.

Viewed in the context of the totality of European history and the idea of reason of state, human rights inescapably are seen not as universal moral principles leading to the good life but as political principles which are in tension with the highest existing effective political order. To assert this is not to dismiss the validity of the pursuit of human rights nor to argue that the lives of millions of people around the world quite possibly would be vastly improved through institutionalizing human rights. It is rather to place in context a discussion worthy of the most dedicated thought and reflection. However fossilized such ancient concepts as "reason of state" may appear, modern man continues to live in a world of sovereign states. The international community is half-organized and, in the words of one observer, semi-anarchic. The nation state for at least half of the world may have outlived its usefulness but no wholly viable form of political organization has appeared to take its place. To recognize the nation state as the controlling political reality for all aspects of war and peace except human rights is to do mankind a disservice and plant seeds of disillusionment and despair. For champions and critics alike of the campaign for human rights the beginning of wisdom is a recognition that tensions exist between human rights and national sovereignty.

2. THE INTERESTS AND OBJECTIVES OF STATES

Whatever may occasionally be possible for enlightened policymakers, most foreign policies then are based on the interests and objectives of nation states. National interest is a produce of the historic objectives of states, their geographic and material position regionally and worldwide and the cooperation of friends and allies whose interests and objectives are convergent. Spokesmen for the national interest are often the objects of criticism from those who impugn their approach as being amoral and cynical yet crimes against humanity more often have been committed by messianic leaders who engaged in political crusades to change the world in their image.

The concept of the national interest has tended to bring restraint and limitations to the conduct of foreign policy. For example, the interests and objectives of the American republic going back to the founders were limited and well-defined. The purpose of American foreign policy so defined was to provide for the security of the "proven territories" of the republic expanding by the mid-19th century from the Atlantic to the Pacific and from north to south reaching to the borders of Mexico and Canada. National security to the south was dependent on the prevention of expansion by any major European power into the Western Hemisphere.

The twin objectives for American foreign policy, therefore, were a preponderance of power in the Western Hemisphere and a balance of power elsewhere in the world. The threat if it came would come from a major outside power and this meant a European power given the preponderance of great powers within Europe and the proximity of Europe to the bulge of Brazil in the Southern Hemisphere. Outside the Western Hemisphere, the interest of the United States was to protect American citizen's engaged in commercial and educational activities abroad. The calculus of foreign policy then was relatively simple and self-contained; for the three Virginians (Jefferson, Madison and Monroe) who succeeded in formulating a rational foreign policy expressed in the Monroe Doctrine the first rule of such a policy was to keep power and commitments in balance. If others outside the Western Hemisphere were to follow American leadership, it was by imitating the example which the United States offered to the rest of the world by the success of its efforts at home. Obscured from the public was the role of the British Navy which through its control of the Atlantic safeguarded American shores from imperialist adventurers.

The shift from a limitationist concept of American foreign policy began with President William McKinley who prayed for divine guidance on the annexation of the Philippines and not unexpectedly received approval for the nation's "manifest destiny" and President Woodrow Wilson who combined world leadership with a moralistic crusade for universal democracy. From Wilson to the present, the most urgent task for policy-makers has been to match political rhetoric with deeds. Forgotten from time to time has been the axiom that leaders ought not to make declarations they were not prepared to defend. Critics such as Walter Lippmann and Lord Keynes pointed out that European states had specific interests and territorial objectives at the Paris Peace Conference after World War I but President Wilson spoke only the language of a towering but vague internationalism. After World War II, the Soviets pursued definite territorial ambitions but the United States fought the war for unconditional surrender and creation of a new international organization which was to bring an end to the balance of power and spheres of influence. Hesitantly and belatedly, the United States fashioned a postwar response to the Soviet threat through policies leading to the Marshall Plan, NATO, an Inter-American Security System, and the Truman Doctrine. The latter, despite the pragmatic approach of its principle architect, George F. Kennan, was formulated more as a universal crusade against the spread of communism everywhere in the world and less as a rational foreign policy calculating means and ends. By the 1970s, it became increasingly clear as demonstrated in the tragedy which befell the Hungarian freedom fighters, in the Nixon Doctrine, in Baskets 1 and 2 of the Helsinki accord and decisively in Vietnam that even so mighty a power as the United States suffered constraints because of its worldwide interests and objectives and the limitations of its national and international power.

3. THEOLOGICAL AND CULTURAL PERSPECTIVES

Innumerable theologians who write and speak on ethics and foreign policy go back to Reinhold Niebuhr.

The Moral Marginalist Perspective: Professor Jerald Brauer observes that when Niebuhr's influence was at his height the danger was moralism, but today it may be cynicism (significantly, Niebuhr always stressed the tension between idealism and realism and spoke of the margins of idealism and realism emphasizing the margins of idealism.) Blueprinting in history is impossible, for both our problems and their solutions are organic, yet leaders have the choice of acting creatively at the margins. While "the field of politics is not helpfully tilled by moralists," and large groups are incapable of love for one another, President Carter on accepting the nomination of his party quoted and added to Niebuhr's words [Carter's addition are in brackets]: "Love must be [aggressively] translated into [simple] justice." Niebuhr also held that "justice means giving each man his due," and the operative principles of justice are liberty and equality. Such principles are operative but not controlling.

Nevertheless, the concept of "moral margins" offers at least the rudiments of an alternative framework to those of reason of state and national sovereignty. It can help man escape from moral cynicism; it offers the possibility of transcendence. It invites studies of other cultures seeking for points of congruence.

Dr. William Bradley, having searched in vain among the world religions for common moral principles as guides to foreign policy, has introduced the concept of the model statesman. Modern western systems tend to vest authority in institutions; some non-western and most ancient ones vest it in their leaders. Their great secular leaders have qualities that exemplify the best in their traditions: the ability to use power without abusing it, to remain humble despite lofty status, to secure and sustain the lives of those under their authority, to practice integrity in all affairs of state, to be even-handed in the administration of justice, to have compassion for the powerless, and to have a sense of personal objectivity. Each civilization and each nation, including some western ones, has such a model of the great ruler to hold up to those who come to power. Therefore, while we may have no concrete answers as they apply to human rights in authoritarian governments, Bradley asserts:

> Insofar as we are able in good conscience to affirm that we are attempting to live by the model of the exemplary leader which is provided by our religious tradition, we have the right to ask those who govern other nations with whom we have dealings to attempt to live by the comparable model set forth by their tradition.

Bradley concludes:

> Perhaps it is better that we should have such models rather than rule books to guide us in a world so rapidly changing as our own. Perhaps the best we can ask is that those in political authority take seriously their religious heritage and make decisions which accord with the highest

standards in their tradition, weighing carefully the consequences of their actions as they intersect with the actions of the leaders of other nations. (Paper, 1977 Conference).

However one searches out the "moral margins," it is an idea with its own pitfalls. All too often the moralist finds the margins in ideals that in a given historical period are seized on as simple moral solutions. Especially when the regnant idea of international morality (outlawry of war, world federalism or human rights) corresponds to our own interests and values, we forget Niebuhr's warnings: "We must never deify freedom. It is not God. It is not even an 'absolute virtue.'"

4. THE INTERNATIONAL POLITICAL SYSTEM

Most of the differences in competing perspectives of world politics result from opposing views of the international political system. Those who adopt the traditional diplomatic perspective see the world as a pluralist system. Not only do nations differ but their differences ought to be preserved. Each has sovereign rights within its territorial boundaries to fashion its own institutions. Each has a cultural tradition, political interests and objectives and its own languages, nationality and history. Even the Charter of the United Nations, the one comprehensive and universal international organization, recognizes this in Article 2, Paragraph 7, which specifies that other nations or organizations are not to intrude on a nation's domestic jurisdiction. The sovereign nation state enjoys impermeability from intervention from without or insurgency or conspiracy from within promoted by an outside power. The nation state is more than a passing phrase in the history of the international system. For all practical purposes, it will continue to be the major operational factor in international politics for the foreseeable future and its independence and autonomy must be respected. No nation nor any international organization is justified in seeking to transform or alter it and whenever attempts are made they are expressions of moral arrogance.

Adherents to the legal approach question almost all these assumptions of the pluralist world view. They maintain that the international system is in the process of being transformed and common or worldwide interests are supplanting national ones. The concept of the national interest is too restrictive and needs to be broadened to take account of expanding transnational activities. International treaties such as the Charter of the United Nations and the Declaration of Human Rights have granted legitimacy to worldwide endeavors and concerns. The nation state is no longer capable of fulfilling mankind's urgent demands for security, welfare and self-fulfillment. In consequence, an emerging universality not pluralism characterizes the international system and with common objectives nations will more and more move toward a monolithic world order.

According to the proponents of a theological perspective, the world order is both universal and pluralistic, universal because the great world religions each partake of some measure of universality and pluralistic because the political order is fragmented into a multi-state system in which religion to some degree and political loyalties absolutely are shaped by the sacred and secular loyalties of the ruler and the state. Yet theologians argue that the existence of two orders makes possible living in two realms which the ancient theologians called the City of God and the city of man. When theologians speak of reaching out for policies which may be found at the moral margins, they envisage the policy-maker reaching up on a vertical plane to approximate horizontally in politics values which are found in a spiritual realm. Theologians call on people to bring pressure to bear on administrations to transcend the national interest. Robert Kennedy used a theological vocabulary in calling on his critics to press the search for policies at the moral margins.

5. THE MUTUALITY OF NATIONAL INTERESTS AND A REALISTIC MORALITY

If there is one object lesson that emerges from a discussion of ethics and foreign policy it is that an ethical position depends on the responsibilities a man carries and on the traditions from which he speaks. Concepts of right and wrong in international relations are overwhelmingly, though not exclusively, the result of national traditions, loyalties and interests. The nation state is both the problem-child of international relations and the highest *effective* expression of genuine moral consensus.

Morality within the nation, as even more dramatically within the family, can be manageable, convincing and attainable. The parent or child in the family brings moral concerns within an acceptable attention-span and focuses energy, devotion and resources on doing what is right for close family members. In much the same way, the moral content of the national interest tends to be more immediate, measurable and personalized while the international interest is more remote, vague and ill-defined. Moreover, the national interest at its best finds expression in various positive formulations. The interest of a nation's people in basic values and the general welfare may be an antidote to ethnic or sectional particularism and crass materialism. A citizenry that takes its history and tradition seriously assures that its reputation will not perish nor its will to survive be destroyed. The sense of membership and of partnership with ancestors who have gone before and heirs who are to follow gives more vitality and political stamina to a nation. In a period of crisis in British politics, Winston S. Churchill counselled his fellow Conservatives: "We are Party men but we shall be all the stronger if in every action we show ourselves capable, even in this period of stress and provocation, of maintaining the division—where there is division—between national and party interests." We have de Tocqueville's statement that "the principle of self-interest rightly understood appears . . . the best suited of all philosophical theories to the wants of the men of our time, and . . . as their chief remaining security against themselves." National interest so understood can guard men against reckless and moralistic crusades and secure a more tolerable relationship between nations each of whom speaks in its national interest rather than claiming to speak for the whole world.

At the same time, nations, while defending the moral integrity of their traditions and interests, ought never to see them exclusively as ends in themselves. World patterns are too complex and variegated for a single state or course of action. The periods of greatest decline in international morality have come when national purposes have been presented as pure and perfect goals for imitation and acceptance by the rest of the world. Nevertheless, there are important areas of foreign policy where national interests must be asserted confidently with courage and pride. Americans run the risk of alternately feeling shame over the fact that we are a great power with a noble tradition and shrinking back in self-abnegation

and dismay when not everyone loves us. American national purposes and policies will be more honored and esteemed if we are
somewhat more humble about equating them with final and absolute virtue. They can be justified as necessary and proper steps in
world affairs without casting them in the form of crusades and
filling the air with the most extravagant claims.

Beyond this, there is something more to foreign policy than
solitary national interest. The one thing that saves the national
interest from itself is its essential reciprocity. Edmund Burke
declared: "Nothing is so fatal to a nation as an extreme of self-
partiality, and the total want of consideration of what others
will naturally hope or fear." As in all human relationships to put
oneself in another's shoes is the most difficult yet essential task of
diplomacy.

It is also true that moral choices are broadly determined by
where we stand within the nation and the world. It makes all the
difference for men and nations, North or South, whether they are
rich or poor, secure or threatened, beneficiaries or victims of the
status quo, defenders or critics, ins or outs, moralists or trimmers,
private or public ethicists, diplomatists or lawyers, urban or rural
people, democrats or communists, absolutists or relativists, liberals
or conservatives, ideologues or pragmatists, nationalists or internationalists, reformers or neo-orthodox. There is no single moral
framework; and for every participant we need to examine assumptions, responsibilities, and power and their connections, coherence,
and inner consistency. In the real world, ethics, politics, and foreign policy intermingle and affect one another; and for every
moral and political act the consequences outweigh and override
good, bad or ambiguous intentions. "By their fruits ye shall know
them" is an ancient but enduring Biblical truth.

6. HUMAN RIGHTS POLICIES AND THE THREE PERSPECTIVES

Of the three perspectives discussed above, each approaches the
promotion of human rights with positions that reflect its assumptions about the international political system and world politics.
The moral framework from which the clearest defense of human
rights emerges is that of the theologians. For this group, no other

policy initiative illustrates more dramatically "acting creatively at the moral margins." Professor Brauer explains that in his head he recognizes the need for prudence in pushing human rights, but in his heart he favors the government's right to act firmly and aggressively. It was necessary to do so, he maintains, for our self-understanding as a people, because concern for racism is worldwide and because the risks of remaining silent outweigh those of speaking out. He prefers not to speak of specific human rights (for example, torture) and the source of our obligation to do something as a government but casts his argument more broadly grounding it in the universality of respect for the sanctity of human life and the rights of the individual everywhere to self-fulfillment. The risk of cynicism is greater today than that of moralism.

The international lawyers are more cautious and warn openly of moral finger-shaking. At the same time, they ask, as did Judge Jessup in a minority opinion of the International Court in the South African case, whether human rights are any longer exclusively matters of domestic jurisdiction. Respect for human rights and fundamental freedoms is now written into such international treaties as the Covenants of Human Rights (the Declaration and the Helsinki agreements are not treaties). The jurists agree, however, that whether an international law principle should be invoked is a matter for policy judgement weighing "putative advantages and risks."

The third perspective, that of the diplomatists, leads inevitably to an attitude of caution and reserve on the subject of human rights. George F. Kennan speaks for this group when he writes:

> To my mind liberty is definable only in terms of the restraints which it implies and accepts. And human rights, too, operate only within a system of discipline and restraint. But if you talk about discipline and restraint you are talking about something that enters into the responsibility of government. Do we, then, in undertaking to decide what "rights" should exist in other countries, propose to tell the people and governments of those countries what restraints should also exist? And can one, then, try to tell another country what rights ought to be observed in its society without telling it what sort of government it ought to have?

Respect for domestic jurisdiction is the keystone of the questioning by the diplomatic analysts of the human rights approach. Routine interference in the essential conduct of one government (that is, its definition of rights and duties) by another is a recipe for political disaster in their relationships. There is little support historically for assuming that moral intervention changes institutions and practices elsewhere; sometimes such intervention can make the situation worse. Given national sovereignty, quiet diplomacy and individual contacts are more likely to yield results. Workability is therefore the companion principle to respect for domestic jurisdiction.

Still diplomatists and students of international politics are not willing to see the people and government of the United States do nothing about human rights. They would have private groups and intellectual and moral leaders speak out; would have us concentrate on being a moral and political example, but not preacher, to others; would urge the government to articulate its beliefs and traditions in broad and general terms (some favored a Gettysburg address by the President as often as it promised to work positive effects); would pick targets of criticism of especially blatant and egregious violations of human rights; would seek ways of orchestrating our views on rights with other essential American goals which at a given moment may be even more important than the human rights campaign (for example, an arms agreement with the Soviet Union); and would urge that any human rights approach be seen as a long run approach toward building consensus and thereby trust for which moral steadiness and political wisdom are more important than a crash program inspired perhaps by moral revulsion to the Kissinger approach and by American domestic politics.

The question that some may ask is does this not lead to moral cynicism. Professor Morgenthau answered by recounting an experience of President Lincoln. At the time of the Civil War, Lincoln was visited by a group of Presbyterian ministers with a petition on the emancipation of the slaves. Lincoln replied to his petitioners by saying that in every great contest each party claims to act on the will of God. Though God cannot be for *and* against the same thing yet each believes he is following the divine will. Lincoln went on that if God had revealed his will to others, one would suppose he would have revealed it to him because of his duties and responsibilities. He was anxious to learn the will of God and to follow it but this is not the day of miracles, he said. He explained he could not do otherwise, therefore, in making moral and political choices than "to study the plain physical facts, ascertain what is possible and learn what is wise and right." Morgenthau describes Lincoln's position as one joining cosmic humility with political realism and urged it as a guide in present circumstances. Though there may be one moral code that men seek, it is filtered through a vast array of moral particularities. The moral code is subject to historical and cultural relativism and, as our lives are precariously poised under the short time fuse of nuclear weapons, to ignore this is to court the destruction of the world.

Presidential Case Studies: Varieties of Moral and Political Experience

William James lives in memory for his study of the varieties of religious experiences. It will come as no surprise, then, that the portraits of modern day Presidents should paint religious outlooks in different colors. For example, the Miller Center of Public Affairs recently published a study entitled *Essays on Lincoln's Faith and Politics* by two authors. One of them, Professor Hans J. Morgenthau, considered that Lincoln was a believing skeptic or skeptical believer "indifferent to religion in dogma and organization [but] ... profoundly and consistently aware of the existential condition from which the religious impulse springs."[1] The other, David Hein, saw Lincoln as a believer holding to a theocentric view of experience.

1. LINCOLN'S FAITH AND POLITICS

Morgenthau's analysis of Lincoln's faith and politics does not stem from any disrespect for religion. Indeed he writes: "The issue that precedes all others both in time and importance is that of religion."[2] For Morgenthau and for Lincoln, religion is not membership in a church or observance of religious practices or professions of faith. It is a religious attitude which recognizes the insufficiency of man as a finite being. It seeks transcendent guidance for man in his relationship with himself, his fellowmen, and the universe. In Morgenthau's words: "Religion is ... a universal human attitude ... of which the historic religions, religious organizations, and religious observances are but particular manifestations."[3] Early in life in 1837, Lincoln wrote to his fiancee, Mary Owens: "I've never been to church nor probably shall not be soon. I stay away myself."[4]

Early in his career, Lincoln running for the Illinois legislature in 1843, was attacked both by opponents of the Episcopal Church and by church members. He defended himself against the former writing to a friend: "It would astonish if not amuse, the older citizens of your County who twelve years ago knew me as a strange(r), friendless, uneducated, penniless boy, working on a flat boat—at ten dollars per month—to learn that I have been put down here as the candidate of pride, wealth and aristocratic family distinction."[5] His opponent was a Campbellite and Lincoln had just married into an aristocratic southern family with Episcopal and Presbyterian ties. Defending himself from the other side, Lincoln found that Christians opposed him "because I belonged to no church, was suspected of being a deist, and had talked about fighting a duel."[6] Significantly Lincoln, having noted these mutually contradictory statements about his religion did not go on to explain which statement was correct.

Three years later, Lincoln running again for the state legislature answered more directly to the charge of his opponent, an itinerant preacher, Rev. Cartright, that he had scoffed at religion. In a "Handbill Replying to Charges of Infidelity," Lincoln replied:

> . . . That I am not a member of any Christian Church, is true; but I have never denied the truth of the Scriptures; and I have never spoken with intentional disrespect of religion in general, of any denomination of Christians in particular. It is true that in early life I was inclined to believe in what I understand is called the "Doctrine of Necessity"—that is, that the human mind is impelled to action, or held in rest by some power, over which the mind itself has no control; and I have sometimes (with one, two or three, but never publicly) tried to maintain this opinion in argument. The habit of arguing thus however, I have, entirely left off for more than five years. And I add here, I have always understood the same opinion to be held by several of the Christian denominations. The foregoing, is the whole truth, briefly stated, in relation to myself, upon the subject.[7]

Lincoln went on to say: "I do not think I could myself, be brought to support a man for office, whom I knew to be an open enemy of, and scoffer at, religion. Leaving the higher matter of eternal consequences, between him and his Maker, I do not think any man has the right thus to insult the feelings, and injure the morals, of the community in which he may live. If, then, I was guilty of such conduct, I should blame no man who should condemn me for it; but I do blame those, whoever they may be, who falsely put such a charge in circulation against me."[8] Morgenthau considers that this statement on religion is not "a particularly fervent or even convincing profession of religious belief." Lincoln was running in 1846 in a rural county in which opposition to religion was tantamount to political suicide. Yet he is negative and defensive about religion, not positive. He says that he doesn't belong to a church, has never denied the scriptures and has not spoken "intentionally" in disrespect of religion. In short, his defense of his religion is that it is not as bad as it has been made out to be. For a politician, his intellectual honesty is striking there not being a single positive assertion of his belief in Christian doctrine. Morgenthau asserts that the name of Christ appears only once in Lincoln's printed writings and that in a purely secular context and that he added the words "under God" to the text of the Gettysburg Address only as he spoke.

Morgenthau discovered one letter by Lincoln to a relative who had written that Lincoln's father was close to death. Of the three such letters Lincoln received informing him of his father's condition, he replied to only one saying of the others: "I could write nothing that could do any good." However he did answer the one in these words:

> I sincerely hope Father may yet recover his health, but at all events tell him to remember to call upon, and confide in, our great, and good, and merciful Maker; who will not turn away from him in any extremity. He notes the fall of a sparrow, and numbers the hairs of our heads; and He will not forget the dying man, who puts his trust in Him. Say to him that if we could meet now, it is doubtful whether it would not be more painful than pleasant; but that if it be his lot to go now, he will soon have a joyous [meeting] with many loved ones gone before; and where [the rest] of us, through the help of God, hope ere-long [to join] them.[9]

Morgenthau reflects on Lincoln's indifference in the face of his father's impending death and suggests that his fervent invocation of God's love could be seen as compensating for his lack of filial love and human feeling. The letter, in any event is only one of two Morgenthau can find in which detachment is replaced by religious fervor in Lincoln's articulation of his faith.

However the story doesn't end at this point. As a statesman, Lincoln was deeply aware of the limits of his knowledge and foresight about events. On April 4, 1864, he declared: "I claim not to have controlled events, but confess plainly that events have controlled me."[10] The sense of dependence on a higher power was not unique to Lincoln. Leaders have sought reassurance through the ages that their acts were in harmony with some divine power. The flights of birds and the entrails of animals gave clues to the divine will. Cromwell at the Battle of Naseby prayed, God smiled on him and he led his troops into battle.

Lincoln was always doubtful that he or any leader had been or could be so blessed. He questioned his ability to understand or influence God's plan. On November 15, 1861, the renowned historian George Bancroft wrote Lincoln declaring that the "Civil War is the instrument of Divine Providence to root out social slavery; posterity will not be satisfied ... unless ... the war shall effect an increase of free states." Lincoln replied in guarded language: "The main thought in ... your letter is one which does not escape my attention, and with which I must deal in all due caution and the best judgment I can bring to it."[11]

Lincoln's careful statement about knowing God's will was made even stronger in his response of September 13, 1862, to a group of Chicago ministers who presented an Emancipation Memorial:

> The subject presented in the memorial is one upon which I have thought much for weeks past and I might even say for months. I am approached with the most opposite opinions and advice and that by religious men, who are equally certain that they represent the Divine will. I am sure that either the one or the other class is mistaken in that belief and perhaps in some respects both. I hope it will not be irreverent for me to say that if it is probable that God would reveal his will to others, on a point so connected with my duty, it might be supposed he would reveal it directly to me; for, unless I am more deceived in myself than I often am, it is my earnest desire

to know the will of Providence in this matter. *And if I can learn what it is I will do it!* These are not, however, the days of miracles, and I suppose it will be granted that I am not to expect a direct revelation. I must study the plain physical facts of the case, ascertain what is possible and learn what appears to be wise and right.[12]

In the Second Inaugural Lincoln portrayed both sides in the Civil War as reading from the same Bible and praying to the same God and went on to say: "The prayers of both could not be answered; that of neither has been answered fully." He had struggled in a private *Meditation on the Divine Will* with the paradox that both sides claimed to be following the will of God and on this he concluded: "Both may be and one must be wrong. God cannot be *for,* and *against* the same thing at the same time."[13] By far his severest indictment was directed at those who argued from self-interest that for *some* people it is better to be slaves and this reflected the will of God:

> Certainly there is no contending against the Will of God; but still there is some difficulty in ascertaining and applying it, to particular cases. For instance we will suppose the Rev. Dr. Ross has a slave named Sambo, and the question is "Is it the Will of God that Sambo shall remain a slave, or be set free?" The Almighty gives no audible answer to the question, and his revelation—the Bible—gives none—or, at most, none but such as admits of a squabble, as to its meaning. No one thinks of asking Sambo's opinion on it. So, at last, it comes to this, that Dr. Ross is to decide the question. And while he consider[s] it, he sits in the shade, with gloves on his hands, and subsists on the bread that Sambo is earning in the burning sun. If he decides that God wills Sambo to continue a slave, he thereby retains his own comfortable position; but if he decides that God wills Sambo to be free, he thereby has to walk out of the shade, throw off his gloves, and delve for his own bread. Will Dr. Ross be activated by that perfect impartiality, which has ever been considered most favorable to correct decisions? But slavery is good for some people!!! As a good thing, slavery is strikingly peculiar in this, that it is the only good

> thing which no man ever seeks the good of, for *himself.*
> Nonsense! wolves devouring lambs not because it is
> good for their own greedy maws, but because it [is] good
> for the lambs!!!¹⁴

Whatever Lincoln's skepticism that men were able to know the
will of God, he could not believe that God willed either slavery or
the destruction of the Union. American slavery was "one of those
offences which in the providence of God . . . He now wills to remove."
Yet Lincoln also believed that God's will as to the time and place
of the ending of slavery was unknown and unknowable. God's
purpose might be different from the purposes of either party. If
God willed that the war continue "until every drop of blood drawn
with the lash, shall be paid by another drawn with the sword . . . the
judgments of the Lord are true and righteous altogether." God
knows best. With a fatalism about God's purposes that matched his
skepticism about knowing God's mind, Lincoln, as the Civil War
continued, told the Baltimore Presbyterian Synod, that he reposed
"reliance in God, knowing . . . that He would decide for the right."[15]
Nevertheless, the fact remains that Lincoln was hesitant about
proclaiming that his policies represented the will of God. God
governs the world by designs that can neither be known nor influ-
enced by man. On October 26, 1862, he wrote to a Quaker lady:

> We are indeed going through a great trial—a fiery
> trial. In the very responsible position in which I happen
> to be placed, being a humble instrument in the hands of
> our Heavenly Father, as I am, and as we all are, to work
> out his great purposes, I have desired that all my works
> and acts may be according to his will, and that it might be
> so, I have sought his aid—but if after endeavoring to do
> my best in the light which he affords me, I find my efforts
> fail, I must believe that for some purpose unknown to me,
> He wills it otherwise. If I had had my way, this war would
> never have been commenced; If I had been allowed my
> way this war would have been ended before this, but we
> find it still continues; and we must believe that He per-
> mits it for some wise purpose of his own, mysterious and
> unknown to us; and though with our limited understand-
> ings we may not be able to comprehend it, yet we cannot
> but believe, that he who made the world still governs it.[16]

Summing up his view of Lincoln's religious philosophy, Professor Morgenthau wrote that "in one sense man is a forlorn actor on the stage of the world; for he does not know the nature of the plot and the outcome of the play written by an inaccessible author. But he is also a confident and self-sufficient actor; for he knows that there is a script, however unknown and unknowable its content, and he can do no more than act out what he believes the script to require."[17]

If Lincoln was a skeptic and a fatalist about religion according to Morgenthau, he was a believer who trusted in the goodness of God for David Hein. The sixteenth President was a "witness to God" who held to a theocentric interpretation of experience. Hein asserts that fatalism "is not an accurate description of [Lincoln's] . . . faith." God was a personal being not an impersonal force. Yet Hein rejects the popular version of Lincoln as a biblical prophet pronouncing the righteous judgments of God upon an immoral and insensitive nation. Nor does he see the War as retribution or a punishment and purging of a people preparing themselves for a new age under God. H. Richard Niebuhr wrote that the judgment that the Civil War brought freedom to the slaves "is questionable, for the war-won liberty of the Negro was not liberty indeed and the equality written into laws was neither complete nor practicable in an uncoverted kingdom of this world."[18]

Thus Hein questions both Morgenthau's view of Lincoln as a skeptic and a fatalist and the views of theologians like Wolf and Endy that Lincoln was God's prophet proclaiming judgment on the basis of what they knew to be God's cause. In Hein's words: "Lincoln did not do any more than forcefully advocate as an imperfect, fallible limited human being the cause he took to be consonant with God's purposes for mankind, acknowledging all the while that he could be wrong, that no special revelation had been vouchsafed to him, that he wanted to forebear judging while working toward his designated, official ends, and that to God alone belonged the credit for accomplishing good."[19] On this question, Hein and Morgenthau are in agreement.

But Hein goes further than Morgenthau in his evaluation of Lincoln's faith. He argues that:

> An appropriate way to understand Lincoln might be
> to see him as a witness to God. We have noted how in his

various efforts as a statesman he kept in mind his duty before God to build community. He fought growing moral indifference to the plight of black men in the 1850s, worked in the war years to preserve the Union and establish the principle of democracy for all the world to see, and perform his tasks without judging his fellow men, giving them up as wicked, or seeking retribution from them. In all this he served as a witness, calling others to dedicate action on behalf of the universal commonwealth, and thereby expressed the active, imperative side of his faith: fidelity to God and to his cause.[20]

Lincoln was a witness to freedom and equality but also to God. He could not persuade himself that he understood the content of God's plan. "He did not know the why of the war but he believed the world to be governed and ordered by Providence.... He did not ... treat the war's afflictions as something glorious ... But neither did he accept the horrors for what they were and reason that God therein was wreaking his vengeance upon the nation. Rather he took the war for the moral evil it was but hoped at the same time that God would accomplish some good even through the strife."[21] Through the suffering of war and the fiery trial, Lincoln saw himself as serving as a witness to God. In holding to this view, Hein offers an alternative interpretation of Lincoln's religion.

2. THE INTERPLAY OF PIETY, POLITICS AND POWER

In turning from Lincoln to other Presidents, writings concerning religious faith take on a different focus. Most Presidents including those who have had strong personal faiths have hesitated to wear their religion on their sleeves. Some may not have thought deeply about their faith. A review of the index of most presidential memoirs turns up few references to religion. Occasionally, the entry "Catholics" or "Jews" appears and this provides a clue to the changing emphasis. Religion in politics has increasingly become an instrument toward the achievement of political ends. Therefore, students are more likely to uncover important evidence on the relationship of religion and politics by examining piety, politics and power than by studying a leader's religion as such.

For one thing, it becomes increasingly difficult to disentangle a leader's public and private religion. For example, what is the average newspaper reader to make of reports that President Reagan seldom goes to church? Is he a deeply religious President who is prevented from going to Church by security considerations? Or does habit play a part as the Rev. Billy Graham, a friend of Presidents since Dwight D. Eisenhower, explained when he said "He has been hindered by the security situation and the fact he didn't always attend church regularly."[22] The Rev. Graham has acknowledged he probably gave the President bad advice in 1981 when he was recuperating from an attempt on his life. As Graham remembers it he told Reagan that "worship of God is disrupted if it becomes a media event." It might have been better, Graham now says, to suggest that the President hold church services in the White House. He is forgiving of the President and says he is sure that he misses church.

Less forgiving are those who accuse Reagan for failing to practice what he preaches. Lou Cannon explains: "He extols religious and family values while rarely going to church or seeing his grandchildren." In recent months, his piety seems directed more at political ends than at radiating an inner faith. However, his former minister, Donn Moomaw, declares: "His faith is very pious and very personal." When Graham called on Reagan in Sacramento, the then-governor asked Graham if he thought the second coming was imminent. How could anyone ask such a question if he had any doubts about God or his own faith, Graham observed.

Nevertheless, it is difficult not to take notice of a shift in Reagan's public use of religion as a political weapon. Cannon writes:

> Most biographers, including this one, have played down the importance of religion in Reagan's life. This may reflect our lack of understanding. But another reason is that Reagan, before yielding to temptations of the political season, treated religion as a private matter. His campaign vow that he would not "wear religion on my sleeve" reflected his basic attitude.[23]

To identify and analyze the shift, Cannon argues, does not deny that Reagan is religious. His intimates say that he prays before making decisions and that he offers spiritual consolation to those who have lost loved ones. He appears to be a compassionate and caring person particularly in traditional areas. Rev. Graham supports this version reminding that "By your fruits shall you know them, not by their church attendance. In his life, we have seen that he bears these fruits."[24]

The change which is being questioned involves not his church attendance but the mixing of religion and politics. Cannon finds that in his religious campaigning of recent months, Reagan has violated an unstated understanding he had with the electorate. Throughout most of his political career he had "conveyed the impression of being a religious man who understood the difference between government and religion. He seemed to recognize he was President of Jews, Roman Catholics, Protestants, secularists, and unbelievers. Now he presumes to speak as an adviser on faith and morals." Now he has joined with fundamentalists and the right wing of his party in pressing the cause of school prayer. He has championed the views of Catholics on abortion and on granting diplomatic recognition to the Vatican. He spoke to a Jewish leader in the fall of 1983 on the coming of Armageddon. He intensified the use of religion in the election year. His actions have caused consternation among those who do not share his religious views while trivialing religious truths for those who do. The admixture of piety and politics disturbs both religious and irreligious groups.

Looking back on the President's vigorous use of religion, Mr. Cannon concludes: "When Reagan cites public opinion polls as a basis for a school prayer amendment and portrays his opponents as less religious than he, he gives the impression that he puts reelection ahead of his faith. What it suggests is not hypocrisy but opportunism. It is a question more bothersome and of greater consequence than any computation of his church attendance."[25]

3. PRESIDENTS AND THE CIVIL RELIGION

Two Presidents in particular reflect elements at least of the nation's civil religion and certain deeply ingrained individual and group characteristics that Americans celebrate: friendliness, boldness and courage, decisiveness, love of family, respect for religion whatever that religion might be, the common touch, energy and sincerity, a record of accomplishment and being a man of action. They are Truman and Eisenhower. Regarding Truman, one White House participant observer describes the handshaking at the Christmas party in 1949 in the Oval House. Having recalled the majesty of Franklin Roosevelt's appearance sitting immobile in his chair, a Truman biographer Ken Hechler writes: "This President [Truman] bobs around and seizes the initiative. He looks like your Uncle Dudley."[26] Truman told the press: "I think the vast majority of you have been as kind to me as I deserve."[27] Dean Rusk once observed that Truman had all the right political instincts mixed with the necessary pugnacity. He kept Winthrop W. Aldrich waiting for a half an hour for an appointment and when he was told by an aide that his wealthy guest seemed agitated, Truman replied: "He's got exactly twenty-two minutes more to wait." He explained that when he was chairman of the Senate War Investigating Committee, "that old S.O.B. made me wait for an hour."[28] Hechler observes: "Truman had a robust Jacksonian attitude toward people. Wealth and power never intimidated him. He had a healthy contempt for those he labeled 'stuffed shirts' or 'prima donnas.' ... A deeply religious person, he had little use for anyone who wrapped a sanctimonious mantle around himself and beat his own chest to proclaim superior piety."[29]

Other traits helps explain Truman's appeal to the ordinary American. He was decisive and the famous sign on his desk, "The buck stops here," was more than a slogan. Hechler notes: "He sensed better than any human being I have ever known precisely when to make a decision and make it stick. There was never any wavering or second-guessing."[30] He was self-educated and knew more American history and world history than his successors. Some of his closest associates were Groton and Yale or Harvard men like Dean Acheson and he remained close to Republicans like Arthur H. Vandenberg and George D. Aiken. He wasn't awestruck by anyone. He reserved his strongest dislikes for wealthy publishers like Scripps and McCormack and politicians like Estes Kefauver and Richard M. Nixon. He bought his own postage stamps for his personal letters and he turned down some of the privileges assigned former Presidents when he left office. He championed the cause of the underdog and, next to his marriage to Bess, the most important event in his life was the birth of daughter Margaret in 1924. He lived out his last days quietly and simply at 219 North Delaware in Independence, Missouri passing away the day after Christmas, 1972, at eighty-eight years of age. Bess died in the autumn of 1982 at the age of ninety-seven. From meeting Bess Wallace in 1890 in Sunday School to their deaths in a mid-west town, the two seemed to personify the virtues of the American civil religion.

So did Dwight D. Eisenhower who followed Truman. The historian Stephen Ambrose writes: "His heritage was ordinary, his parents were humble folk, his childhood was typical of thousands of other youngsters growing up around the turn of the century."[31] He was born in the year the American frontier came to an end. His ancestors were Pennsylvania Dutch, immigrants from the Rhineland. He was raised in a traditional German family in which his father's authority was unquestioned, his mother's love and caring unending. After the boys did the dishes, the family gathered around the father for Bible reading. Ambrose sums up their family background: "Typical parents . . . raising typical kids in a typical small town in the heart of America. . . . They emphasize accomplishment rather than intellectual contemplation . . ."[32]. Even the Bible reading was mechanical and unquestioning. If it taught the children to read the Bible, said Milton Eisenhower, it was not a good way to help understand it. Abilene, Kansas in the 1890s was conservative, Christian and Republican. There was a strong sense of community and a feeling that the world was divided into "us" (Abilene and most of Kansas) and "them" (the rest of the world).

Eisenhower had a temper. When at age ten he was stopped from going "trick or treating" by his parents, he pounded the trunk of an apple tree until his fists were a raw bleeding mass. Years later Bryce Harlow told a Miller Center interviewer that witnessing one of Ike's outbursts was like looking into a Bessemer furnace. After the Halloween outburst, his mother told him that he had much the worst temper of all her boys and explained how futile and self-destructive anger could be. Sixty-six years later Eisenhower remembered his mother's words: "He that conquerth his own soul is greater than he who takes a city." He considered that conversation "one of the most valuable moments in my life."

In preparing the Miller Center Portrait of Eisenhower, we were impressed by the love and respect his associates had for him. They saw him as a man of integrity who sought to bring order and discipline to government. He worked from principles and introduced his subordinates to practical aphorisms such as "never say never" or don't pretend to know the intentions of others as in saying someone "deliberately" did so and so. Despite his own rather parochial background, he was an uncompromising internationalist. Indeed it has been said that he finally chose to run for office because he wasn't sure that Senator Robert A. Taft was an internationalist. Ironically, Eisenhower was probably more conservative domestically than Taft.

Eisenhower's image as an acute and involved political leader has been restored by the revisionist school led by Professor Fred Greenstein of Princeton. What has not changed is the picture of his resolve somehow to stand above politics. He was deeply hurt by the political barbs Truman directed at him in the 1952 campaign, thrusts that were merely part of the game for Truman. He would not lower himself or the dignity of his office to fight in the gutter with Senator McCarthy. In administering the government, he preferred that subordinates to whom he had delegated a task take responsibility and receive the credit in order that they might grow. He surrounded himself with Republicans and Democrats, with scientists as diverse as Kistiakowsky and Teller, and with business leaders like the Wilsons and journalists and writers like Emmet Hughes and Arthur Larson.

In the end, he appeared to have "conquered his own soul" because while the sources and volatility of his anger never disappeared, he learned to listen to widely different views and to employ the give and take of Cabinet government as few Presidents before or since. His energy and vitality never flagged and he could inspire initiative in others. Above all, he made the most of his talents (he had been a somewhat mediocre student). He was less flamboyant than MacArthur or Patton but far steadier and more skillful in maintaining relations with others.

In all his efforts, Eisenhower remained a folk hero for reasons Professor John E. Muller of the University of Rochester has identified and assessed: his personal appeal, one sensational achievement: ending the war in Korea, his amateur status as a politician, his domestic conservatism and his good fortune in coming to office in a period of natural goodness and, I would add to Muller's list, the closeness of his life to the precepts and practices of the civil religion.

4. CORRELATION OF TYPES OF PIETY TO TYPES OF LEADERSHIP AND POWER

A concluding theme is the correlation of types of piety to types of leadership and power. How often have we not heard "he was the right leader for the times." The Truman Era, and especially the famed sixteen weeks of the Truman Doctrine and the Marshall Plan, were a turning point in American foreign policy. A respected liberal figure was needed to carry the public from an era of good feeling with the Russians to a period of containment of Soviet expansionism. It was fortunate that Truman was trusted by congressional leaders especially men like Sam Rayburn and Senator Arthur Vandenberg with whom he shaped a bipartisanship foreign policy. Truman's ties with an informal late afternoon drinking group in the Congress known felicitously as the "Board of Education" must also have been helpful. No less crucial were the men immediately around the President including George C. Marshall, Dean Acheson and Robert Lovett. An insecure President would have shrunk from the appointment of such giants. Harry Truman felt secure dealing with the likes of Marshall, Acheson and Lovett who may all have been his intellectual superiors. Because of the office he held, he was boss. As he told Frank Pace: "As Harry Truman I'm not very much but as President Truman I have no peer."[33]

For James Rowe who knew and worked with five Presidents, Franklin D. Roosevelt "is still the standard to which we should all repair . . . as President." His strengths were political strengths and he needed every ounce of them to deal with the Depression and the Second World War. In Rowe's words: "He was all charm. . . . His staff adored him. In the back room when we were working, his charm would sort of disappear." He disciplined the staff. His other quality, Rowe says, was the fact "as a politician he never tried to get too far ahead of the American people in his judgment."[34] By 1933, as the historian John Norton Blum has put it, "the presidency had lost the stature that Theodore Roosevelt and Wilson had given it." FDR restored that stature and added to it. The times and the crises required a dominating presence, someone whose assurances to the American people were credible when he promised they had "nothing to fear but fear itself." At his first press conference, Roosevelt announced that he would divide what he wanted to say into:

1. statements attributable to him but only in indirect quotation;
2. material for direct quotation which was relatively rare and usually on request of reporters to use, in quotes, some striking phrase;
3. background information that showed up in print under such euphemisms as "the President is known to think that. . . . " and
4. off the record information . . . on individuals or nations that often subtly colored the reporting about both.

At the end of that first press conference, the press broke into applause. No one remembers that ever happening before or since.

What Roosevelt controlled in his press conference (although even he fell prey to a certain hubris when he awarded a hypothetical iron cross to one reporter) was what he controlled throughout his administration. No one else has had the skill to master the political environment quite as fully as he did.

Whatever his personal traits, the piety of the ill-fated Richard M. Nixon was in harmony with the foreign policy leadership requirements of his time. Who but a lifelong crusader against communism could have brought about normalization with China without raising a whimper from the constituency of the so-called Committee of a Million that had spearheaded the resistance to any opening up of relations with Communist China? Who but the champion of the forgotten middle-American middle class could have sought improved relations with the Third World? And who but the defender of the American faith in a Soviet televised debate with Khrushchev could go to the Summit not once but repeatedly even after the mining of Haiphong harbor.

It was Nixon's good fortune that Eisenhower, Kennedy and Johnson had laid the groundwork for detente with the Soviets. He merely continued work that others had begun in meetings at Geneva, Vienna and Glassboro; with Open Skies, test ban and security negotiations. What matters is that Nixon with an agile NSC advisor later Secretary of State was able to continue and extend what others had initiated. The correlation between Nixon's piety and leadership fit the times until Watergate at least.

How ironic that we should come to the end of our discourse

with Richard Nixon. Time and space has robbed us of the chance
to consider Lyndon B. Johnson's roughhewn piety that responded
to civil rights needs with legislation no other President before or
since has matched. Or John F. Kennedy whose all too brief years
helped kindle hope around the world. Or Gerald Ford who brought
a period of healing. Each promises a case study of its own of the
complex relation of faith and politics.

What are the lessons to be drawn? There are too many for
listing here but a few stand out. In politics and diplomacy, *workability* more often than not must be the watchword of a President
striving for popular and party support, rounding up followers like a
sheep dog, organizing coalitions in order to govern, defining the
national interest: the hard, grubby, inescapable business of every
administration. But moral standards also exist sometimes measured by declarations and commitments, other times by style and a
thousand little acts of good will. The Good Neighbor Policy made
a difference but so did Secretary Rusk's reporting to Organization
of American States' Ambassadors immediately after the Cuban
Missile decision. Morality enters foreign policy in the interstices
even when the excuses for conflict are festering. We must live on
this globe, this tiny speck of dust in the universe, however perverse
our rivals may be. Forgiveness of seven times seventy is not a
foreign policy axiom but something approximating it is needed in
the nuclear age. What a commentary that human beings have
achieved their greatest mastery at scoring points on one another
and equipping themselves for lethal conflict. Have we also advanced
far enough, as Herbert Butterfield urged, to take a chance for
peace, not in the sense of giving everything away but precisely
because we are hardboiled realists about the destruction of the
world?

Politics and morality intersect. For Americans the answers are
not set forth in a single text or study or guide book, yet no tradition
is richer overall in its moral and intellectual sources. Curiously, as
Nixon told the Society of Newspaper Editors, "communists are
looking at problems, and we are looking at communists." Perhaps
if we worried less about our rival and its creed and more about
urgent problems, we would end up rediscovering the link between
morality and politics.[35]

NOTES

1. Hans J. Morgenthau and David Hein, *Essays on Lincoln's Faith and Politics*, Washington: University Press of America, 1983, p. 9.
2. *Ibid.*, p. 6.
3. *Ibid.*
4. *Ibid.*, p. 4.
5. *Ibid.*, p. 6.
6. *Ibid.*
7. *Ibid.*, p. 7.
8. *Ibid.*, pp. 7-8.
9. *Ibid.*, p. 9.
10. *Ibid.*, p. 10.
11. *Ibid.*
12. *Ibid.*, pp. 10-11.
13. *Ibid.*, p. 13.
14. *Ibid.*, pp. 11-12.
15. *Ibid.*, p. 13.
16. *Ibid.*, pp. 13-14.
17. *Ibid.*, p. 16.
18. *Ibid.*, p. 106.
19. *Ibid.*, p. 154.
20. *Ibid.*
21. *Ibid.*, p. 155.
22. Lou Cannon, "Reagan & Company," *The Washington Post,* April 16, 1984, A2.
23. *Ibid.*
24. *Ibid.*
25. *Ibid.*
26. Ken Hechler, *Working with Truman,* New York: C. P. Putnam's Sons, 1982, p. 125.
27. *Ibid.*
28. *Ibid.*, p. 15.
29. *Ibid.*, p. 16.
30. *Ibid.*
31. Stephen E. Ambrose, *Eisenhower,* Vol. I, New York: Simon and Schuster, 1983, p. 13.
32. *Ibid.*, p. 23.
33. Kenneth W. Thompson, (ed.) *Portraits of American Presidents: The Truman Presidency,* Vol. II, Washington, D.C.: University Press of America, 1982, pp. 149.
34. Kenneth W. Thompson, (ed.) *Portraits of American Presidents: The Roosevelt Presidency,* Vol. I, Washington, D.C.: University Press of America, 1982, pp. 4-5).
35. This chapter is a modified version of the Stuber Lectures.

The Dilemmas and Antinomies
of Leadership

Whether the problem of leadership is related to the disappearance of heroes and hero worship from society is not altogether clear. The story is told of the senator who was returning from a Washington event and, recalling the people they had met, turned to his wife and said, "Isn't it tragic, darling, that there are so few great men left today?" And she turned to him and said, "There's one less than you think there is, darling."

Another perspective on leadership is the statement of a former colleague who said, when you get into the lion's den either the lion will get you or you will get the lion. The notion of confrontation is illustrative of leadership on the attack. Another approach results from the transposition of phrases or words known to those of you who once had training in Fort Benning, Georgia. You may recall transposing the phrase which was a motto of shining new second lieutenants, "follow me," to read "follow you." It seemed a good deal safer under the circumstances.

1. ANTINOMIES AND CONTRADICTIONS OF LEADERSHIP

A more basic reason, however, that leadership is so complex and so difficult to assess and measure is that almost any proposal regarding leadership presents a series of contradictions, tensions, and antinomies. Any proposition put forward from one standpoint about leadership is almost immediately subject to qualification on the other side of the ledger. Discussions of leadership become a matter of drawing a line down the middle of a page. In thinking about leadership, for every truth there is a balancing truth; in the application of leadership, for everything there is a season. What seems appropriate and effective in one era is less effective in another.

One quickly confronts such issues when he begins to think about some of the commonplace notions of leadership like the concept of the charismatic leader, the spiritual or political figure who captures the people's attention and imagination. In the state of Illinois where I lived for a decade, it was said that one of the great misfortunes for Governor Adlai Stevenson was that discussion never seemed to flow toward and center on him the way it did with charismatic and dynamic leaders. The mass of the people were not drawn to him. It wasn't that he didn't know as much or more than others nor was able to formulate and define issues clearly. But somehow the flow of discussion oftentimes went the other way. He was too reserved and too distant in personal relations. His associations were too formal and abstract. His demeanor ran counter to the image of a magnetic leader. He was lacking in the one area that some considered most essential for leadership. Another perspective on leadership posits the view that what one seeks in a leader is someone who is so average, so common and so mediocre as to appear the same as everyone else. This notion was voiced in connection with the nomination of a Supreme Court Justice not so long ago defended in these terms. We were asked wouldn't you feel better with somebody who was as average as everybody else. In a more elegant and legitimate way Carl Schurz wrote regarding Lincoln as leader, "You are underrating the President. . . . I grant he lacks higher education and his manners are not in accord with European conceptions and the dignity of a chief magistrate. He is a well developed child of nature and is not skilled in polite phrases and prose. But he is a man of profound feelings, correct and firm principles and incorruptible honesty. His motives are unquestionable and he possess to a remarkable degree the characteristic God-given trait of this people, sound commonsense." In that one trait at least, Lincoln was seen as a child of the people.

In any event, the notion of inspiration and charisma is in tension with the notion of the leader as someone close to the people and not all that different from them. A similar tension exists between certain other elements of greatness. A former colleague at his death left an unpublished manuscript on Lincoln as leader. The first chapter is devoted to the greatness of Lincoln. Professor

Hans J. Morgenthau asks in his treatise what is greatness in any man and more particularly what is greatness in a statesman? He quotes Emerson on the uses of great men who wrote, "he is great who is what he is from nature and never reminds us of others."[1] He discusses uniqueness in the statesman and then goes on to compare it with uniqueness in other areas. Babe Ruth was a great baseball player, Pierpont Morgan a great banker, etc. These men were great because they pushed one particular human faculty, whether physical prowess, culinary creativity or acquisition of money to the outer limits of human potentiality; they developed one human faculty to perfection. Then Hans Morgenthau comments, "But this is a limited greatness of a functional nature. A man is called great because he performs a particular function to perfection."[2] There is a difference between a great baseball player, a great chef, and so on and Emerson points to this difference when he writes of a great man that he must be related to us. Our life receives from him some promise of explanation. That is to say, a great man, in contrast to a man performing a particular function greatly, is one who at least approaches perfection in certain qualities of mind, character, and action that illuminate the very nature of man. He not only illuminates the nature of man but also holds up a mirror to his aspirations. He demonstrates in actual experience how far man can go and hence how much farther than he thought was possible a man can go who at least aspires to be great. "Great men," Emerson wrote, "speak to our wants."

Morgenthau goes on to argue that in these terms Lincoln appears indeed as a great man, of unique greatness combining within himself perfection of human potentialities to be found in such combination in few other men known to history. And he treats his statesmanship as greatness independent of success or failure. The unadorned qualities of his greatness have tended to disappear or at least become indistinct in the fact of mythological interpretations, but they persist in certain qualities which become the subject of Professor Morgenthau's book and of his analysis.[3] Yet on the other side, effective leadership seems to involve something in which uniqueness, if it is present, has to remain somehow credible. When I worked in New York one of the discussions in the early years of the Civil Rights movement was whether Ralph Bunche was in fact a leader for blacks and an example for other young aspiring minorities. The issue was whether Ralph Bunche was so far removed and so distant from the aspirations of the ordinary black that in fact he gave them no leadership; looking at him gave them no example for their lives.

Further, in this general introductory profile of the main characteristics and major aspects of leadership, one should say something about the mystery of leadership. The person who said it best in his writings is Sir Harold Nicolson, especially in the *Portrait of a Diplomatist* which is an account of his father. Drawing on a portrait furnished by his daughter-in-law, he records that his father, Sir Arthur Nicolson, who was himself a diplomat, was: "Although physically so small and fragile, his manner was conceived upon a scale of ample but authoritative courtesy. He was impressive not insignificant. With all his gentleness, all his simplicity he contrived to impose his personality."[4] One is reminded of the pianist Arthur Rubenstein who was asked what is the first thing you do in a concert and he answered, "My first act must be to impose my presence upon the audience." Sir Arthur Nicolson in turn imposed his personality so that in a company of several people it was of his presence that one remained aware and to him that one naturally deferred. "He might sit silent in his arm chair watching, trying to hear, for he was growing deaf, but one could never forget that he was there. This quality must be due, one inevitably thought, to something essential in the man himself."[5] I used to wonder, Harold Nicholson wrote, what "is at the root of one's deference, respect and affection? For in spite of his irreproachable manners and his charm he is aloof, slightly unreal, removed from life by reason of his age, his disabilities and his absentmindness which come over him as he grows tired." But the answer was not hard to find. "It is not often," the son concluded, "that one meets a man whose absolute goodness and integrity proclaim themselves in the first glance of his eyes, as one first shakes hands, not often that one feels compelled to acknowledge the moral attributes as a basis of personal impression. Thus, however, it was with him. One's perception of him was most curiously and vividly compounded of physical compassion and spiritual homage."[6] Not surprisingly, Sir Harold Nicolson wrote these words in the language of the classics speaking of virtue, of goodness and of the good man. I remember talking well into the morning hours with Leo Strauss about his proposition that as you moved into any group you could somehow identify the person who had a kind of intrinsic or inherent goodness or virtue and that virtue might well have been a product of his self-fulfillment within the processes of social life and political life according to Strauss.

Yet this notion of the visible leader stands in tension with the notion of leadership which appears, although in different language and formulation in various discussions and papers. The leader is antileader; it is a characteristic of the leader that he conceals or downplays the fact he is leading. As an example, we are in the midst today of a revisionist trend of thought and writing about President Dwight D. Eisenhower and the "hidden hand" form of leadership which Eisenhower, according to Professor Fred Greenstein, practiced. He led but literally concealed his leadership from those who were trying to interpret his leadership. The example that comes most readily to mind is the McCarthy episode and Ike's refusal to speak out in support of General Marshall from a campaign train platform in Wisconsin. There is another antileader of course, a little bit less popular in some quarters, represented by Calvin Coolidge of whom it was said by Alice Roosevelt Longworth, that "the unsmiling Coolidge had been weaned on a pickle." Somebody else observed in the twenties that, "the American people wanted nothing done and Cal obliged them completely." And another observed in a more kindly vein that "he had no ideas but he was not a nuisance." This vision of leadership surely stands in contradistinction with the mystery of an all pervasive leadership.

2. ATTRIBUTES OF LEADERSHIP

If we go on to assess the most important attributes of leadership, the same tensions and antinomies are evident. What are some of the attributes of leadership in the political sphere, if one can enumerate them while leaving a more complete analysis to others? In political terms, one attribute is the role of the leader as unifier, harmonizer, and coalition builder. The Miller Center undertook a review of the presidential nominating process and invited testimony from former presidential candidates and their aides. A common bond that united George McGovern and the people who were responsible for the reforms of the nominating process in the late sixties and early seventies with conservatives on the far right was that they agreed that the nominating process as it presently exists virtually guarantees that a president would come to office without a coalition to govern. If you divest the nominating process of participation by those who possess the capacity which former Congresswoman Edith Green described as "having a sense of what is possible and practical," then you bring a leader to office without the means of governing and without the capacity of pursuing his policies with the support of an effective political coalition. In fact, President Jimmy Carter's failure was largely a result of this lack.

So a President ought to be a leader, a harmonizer, a unifier and a coalition builder. But what about the situation where his task is to move the country ahead? What about the need for the President to be an antagonist as against the idea of his being a harmonizer? The person who, I suppose, best illustrated the role of antagonist was the old curmudgeon, Harold Ickes, who within the Roosevelt administration continually pressed and pushed, with very little help from others, for ideas which found their way into legislation. How do you resist special interests if your only task is to harmonize? Therefore, the two attributes of the leader as unifier and antagonist seem, at least provisionally, to be in tension.

Almost all government textbooks refer to political courage as the master virtue in politics, the ability to make decisions. A decision is something different from an opinion. A decision can't be put in a desk drawer and looked at a year or a day from now. People are required to stand up and make choices. But how does the quality of decisiveness relate to the need we all feel for a normalizer particularly in certain circumstances? Walter Lippmann with all his preference for most of the ideas for which Adlai Stevenson stood, nevertheless came out in support of Dwight Eisenhower for President because he said Eisenhower could restore the country to a sense of normality and stability within its boundaries. He could restore people's self-confidence and satisfaction with themselves and their government. In that sense, lowering the temperature, slowing the pace at a certain moment in the cyclical movement of politics when the American people have grown weary and fatigued, either after a war or after a great leap forward in some social area, is considered essential. Gerald Ford after Watergate seemed to perform this function.

Another attribute of the leader is the attribute of judgment. I have a Charlottesville friend who describes her late husband as having a single dominant virtue and that was the virtue of judgment.

She says others were brighter, more handsome, had more money; but her husband had judgment and the people of Charlottesville all knew it. This is not too far removed from what political theory teaches about leadership. Because acting in the context of politics puts a high premium on what an Indonesian friend, Soedjatmoko, has called sheer blind groping, judgment is vital.[7] In the making of political choices, the process is different from the process in which most of us engage most of the time as we seek for clarity in the intellectual, philosophical and scholarly area. Decision making involves the process of allowing facts, events and trends to wash over you, to listen for the rustle of the tide of events and then to grab hold of the garments of history as it moves past. It involves settling for some more or less harmful alternative in making a choice that has to be made. Thus judgment involves seeking for coherence and making the right choice. Those people who worked most closely with Harry S. Truman talked about his decisiveness, as the journalists did, but they talked about something else that in a way is even more significant. They said—and these were intellectuals like Acheson and many others—that he seemed to have all the right instincts for the choices that had to be made. It was his instincts somehow, apart from pure rational deduction, that guided him to the right choice.

Yet if one carries this too far, if one reminds his wife when she wants to decide immediately on a matter to wait awhile and think twice about a decision, then the fate of Hamlet may be upon us. There is risk in the temptation to postpone decisions in order that one's judgment be improved. There are dangers in allowing history to overwhelm or pass over the decision maker. So the antinomy of the process of measured judgment, as I have described it, is the process of waiting too long. The historian, Walter Johnson, with all his faith and fervor regarding Adlai Stevenson, nevertheless at the end of his biography comes down rather hard on Stevenson and his Hamlet-like quality. In defense of Stevenson, Johnson cites examples of the prison strike in Springfield when Stevenson was decisive and in command. Yet one almost senses in Johnson a protest that is too strong and too shrill.[8] Quincy Wright, who taught in Chicago and Virginia, never tired of telling a story regarding General Eisenhower. When Wright was an advisor at the Nuremberg trial, he needed money for some activity. He went to Eisenhower and said we can't go on with the consulting we are doing without

money and he was sure that this would open up a long bureaucratic process. Eisenhower picked up the phone, reported Professor Wright, and announced that Wright and his colleagues needed
such and such funds to carry on their work. As Wright walked out
the door, somebody handed him an envelope containing the money.

Thus tensions exist between certain forces and one struggles to
reconcile them. President Reagan has talked again and again about
simplifying. He has said there is a tendency for intellectuals and
those who write about policy to needlessly complicate problems
which at root and with regard to essentials are basically simple. To
the extent he has succeeded in certain policy areas, this quality of
simplification is a strength for him in communication. However
there is a taint of anti-intellectualism in this view but also an
element which within a democracy has some appeal. It was James
Fallows who complained that President Carter was endlessly disposed to write every speech for the service station operator. H. L.
Mencken once wrote "for every human problem there is a solution
which is simple, comforting and wrong." These perspectives on
politics have thrown the notion of simplifying into question. The
trivialization and falsification of reality in politics seems to be the
product of too much simplification. Television coverage based on
a thirty-second or sixty-second encapsulation of the truth may
leave one as far from the truth as one was before viewing the
thirty-second capsule.

Another attribute of leadership involves conveying hope. Whatever anyone says in dispargement of President Reagan, he appears
to have given some people hope. One reason the incumbent came
to office, we're told, was because in contrast with Jimmy Carter he
offered hope. But what about the other side. What about the
Pollyannish depiction of reality when that reality has a major
element of tragedy about it. Doesn't false hope contain inherent
elements of failure? Don't ongoing problems require sacrifice?
What about the disillusionment that follows the illusion which an
effort at false or imaginary hope creates? The Norman Vincent
Peale of politics is not always the leader with the most lasting
impact. Yet the literature on politics by many political scientists
has criticized politicians, including Mr. Carter, who are said to
offer too little hope.

There are other attributes in politics, one being detachment,
that are discussed in the substance of the essay on Lincoln from

which I have quoted. Kennedy possessed a sense of detachment with his self-mockery. Lincoln perhaps had it at a more profound level with his objectivity. He had a capacity somehow, even in the midst of a Civil War, to view the conflict as though he was looking at it from the other side of the battle lines as well as his own. He had the same objectivity and detachment with regard to himself and his personal appearance. He had it when he came to Washington after his election and was serenaded. What did he say to the serenaders? He responded, "I suppose I may take this as a compliment paid to me and as such please accept my thanks for it. I have reached the city of Washington under circumstances considerably differing from those under which any other man has reached it. I have reached it for the purpose of taking an official position amongst the people almost all of whom were opposed to me and are as yet opposed to me, as I suppose."[9] Imagine any other President who has just been elected in the face of a threatening rebellion on behalf of slavery coming into the District of Columbia where slavery is legal and finding himself serenaded by the supporters of slavery. Lincoln didn't try to gloss over the situation. He didn't offer any concessions nor did he ask for any from his audience. On the contrary, by defining the situation in all its unique starkness, he emphasized its absurdity. He looked at himself, he looked at the crowd and their mutual relations and not only recognized but also articulated his extraordinary position with objectivity saying, "I am alone, you are against me."

Consider the Civil War which saddled him with the crushing burden of enormous bloodletting, with long drawn out conflict, overwhelming the nation with all its international and domestic repercussions and all in good measure the result of the incompetence of some of the leaders, including the generals. On July 1st, Lincoln called for three hundred thousand volunteers using the phrase—and can anyone imagine a present day leader using a similar phrase—"so as to bring this unnecessary and injurious civil war to a speedy and satisfactory conclusion."[10] Imagine any President fighting a war, widely regarded to be unnecessary and injurious, calling for volunteers to fight it. Would he not appeal to the people to fight a necessary and beneficial war in order to obtain the maximum beneficial response? One can give even more telling examples of this spirit of detachment with regard to the interpretation of the struggle itself, the Civil War. This sympathy reflected itself in his attitudes toward deserters when he struggled with himself and with the law in trying in some more detached way to come to what he thought was an approximation of justice.

You may say, if this is the quality of leadership, what about enthusiasm for a cause? If detachment is a quality of leadership, what about the need for passion, what about the need for conviction and for taking a position which will inspire response by the people? Is there not an intrinsic tension between these two qualities which seem essential to success in politics? One writer has written of objectivity in observing a political situation that what is required of the statesman is to see clearly: first, to see his country and himself, then the situation of his rival, then that situation as his rival sees it, then his own situation as the enemy sees him. To see clearly means to see without passion, without the passion of pride, of hatred and of contempt. The statesmen must somehow master the paradox of wanting passionately to triumph over an enemy, to dominate that enemy to whom he feels passionately superior yet at the same time having to view his relations with that rival or enemy with the sense of detachment and objectivity which Lincoln attained.

3. THE TOOLS AND CONSTRAINTS OF LEADERSHIP

Let me treat two other issues briefly. One concerns the tools of the leader, the requirements of leadership. Top administrative officials who have served with a particular chief executive and been particularly close to him have stressed the role of the leader as sheepdog, the person within a democracy who rounds up followers who are more and more stubbornly resistant. My colleague, James S. Young, refers to the crisis of leadership as essentially the crisis of followership. The necessary ongoing, unremitting struggle to bring people on line through word and deed is an essential characteristic of leadership and of the requirements of leadership. Yet, others talk of leadership and of the requirements of leadership as involving the action of those who sound the clarion call. The leader is the trumpeter, the person who points the way. I'll come back to that.

How is one to fix these elements, these requirements of leadership in relationship to one another? In considering the tools and constraints of the leader, how is one to relate to the role of mastery of the last detail with commanding a grand design or comprehensive plan in order that those who are followers avoid a sense of drift and purpose? I once went to work for a man who had four different sized note pads alongside his desk, each larger than the other.[11] I thought this was the most unnecessary and ostentatious administrative action I had ever seen. But then I got to know him and I realized that each pad was there to note certain things that had to be done: big things or little things, inside things or outside things, dealing with junior colleagues or senior colleagues. I can't remember all the distinctions. But he used his administrative props and supports with great skill. He was stronger as a leader than many people with whom I worked because he succeeded in keeping the details in mind. It is appropriate to mention the Carter White House oral history project conducted by the Miller Center. Several of the participants, particularly the young people who came to Washington with President Carter, have remarked about the enormous burden of the pressures of their work. Several of them have said, "Do you know that on certain days we get as many as twenty or thirty, even as many as fifty telephone calls. We never had that in other things we did."[12] Yet anyone who has had some degree of responsibility isn't for a moment surprised that one should get fifty telephone calls. The telephone calls simply chart the unending flow of demands and pressures by which one may be overwhelmed if one takes charge of events or if one lets them trouble and perplex him too much.

A friend from an earlier period who was second or third in command in the State Department had his secretary keep a stopwatch on him during a period of service. He wanted to learn how long he directed his attention to any given subject. The secretary found that the average time he gave during a working day to a single subject was two minutes. In a position where a succession of decisions are required, the flow of action, the flow of questions and requests, or little and big steps that have to be taken is so enormous that the person who thinks that he can master them all by working half time at the task is likely to be overwhelmed. However much we question the importance of being on the job and of working on details, one finds that something not attended to can lead to the breakdown of many, many good ideas. Woodrow Wilson was probably intellectually and morally superior to Lloyd George and Clemenceau in Paris measured by his vision, fervor and convictions. Yet Wilson cared not at all for the details of territorial settlements. He saw them as something that might be reached through cynical negotiations that lay outside the first duty of the President. However, those who had mastered the details at the Paris Peace Conference, who knew the historic background of states and regions and the demands of national groups were in a superior position in writing the treaty. Yet on the other hand, the person too immersed in detail, the person with no vision and no direction falls short of the man with vision. Hence the antinomy and the conflict. Winston Churchill asked at the beginning of one of his volumes why did we stumble into the First World War? Having looked at various reasons he answered his own question by saying "we had no plan." The West had no conception of what was required for achieving a concentration of power to resist power. We had no plan for using that power creatively and effectively through diplomacy. It is interesting that throughout his career Churchill constantly linked power and negotiations in a way that few statesmen have done. This was his grand design or plan if you will, something more than a collection of details.[13]

Another tension is the tension between private leadership, private diplomacy, executive privilege, and public responsibility. This subject runs the gamut of almost every issue one is likely to explore including the settlement of disputes and the mediation of sharp differences. All of these issues obviously lend themselves best to some kind of private diplomacy and private settlement. But at the same time, many writers of note have called attention to the issue of accountability. On April 9, 1982, Admiral Rickover was a guest of the Miller Center.[14] He was somebody who throughout his military career made a religion out of accountability. He apparently would say to all of his subordinates, "I'm not going to judge what you do in this action or that action, but I'll judge you in terms of your accountability. I'm going to judge you as to whether you accomplish what you are asked to do and in accordance with the tasks you are called upon to carry out." Obviously, his idea was the notion writ large of public responsibility and accountability.

One or two final attributes involve the tension between ideas and pervade discussions of leadership. Those people who were leaders seem to have been able to package answers to problems and seem to have had ideas about the management of such matters. They were more than mere technicians. They had a theory or philosophy. On the other hand, we have it from perhaps the most monetarily successful writer about his public service career, Henry Kissinger, that one doesn't get any new ideas once one takes on responsibility in the public service. One must live on the intellectual capital which he brings to the office.

How does one connect and relate all these issues? How does one measure them and what is one to think about the proposition regarding presidential leadership by someone who lays it down, though without any great certainty, that "it is the President who sets the tone, helps to shape moods and expectations and provides or fails to provide a framework for public understanding?" Of all the words that I have written, I think I have gotten more comment pro and con on that statement. On the one side, many of the presidential scholars say, "How do you expect a chief executive to set the tone, to help public understanding or to provide a framework? That isn't his responsibility." The task of the successful President is to be elected, to fashion a coalition and to institute a successful legislative program. But that wasn't what the Founders said. The Founders thought that it also was the task of the President to do certain other things. I suppose the question with which we begin in our discussion of leadership and predictably end is whether or not, in various spheres of leadership this function that I have just described is a necessary and realizable function of the leader.

NOTES

1. Hans J. Morgenthau and David Hein, *Essays on Lincoln's Faith and Politics,* edited by Kenneth W. Thompson, (Washington, D.C.: University Press of America, 1983) 3-4.
2. Ibid., 4.
3. Ibid.
4. Sir Harold Nicolson, *Portrait of a Diplomatist,* (Boston: Houghton Mifflin, 1930), 315-16.
5. Ibid., 316.
6. Ibid.
7. Soedjatmoko is President of the United Nations University and his writings and speeches are regularly published in the publications of the University.
8. Walter Johnson, *How We Drafted Adlai Stevenson.*
9. Morgenthau, op. cit., 19-20.

10. Ibid.
11. The man was Dr. Joseph H. Willits, Director of Social Sciences at the Rockefeller Foundation who had been Dean of the Wharton School of Finance at the University of Pennsylvania.
12. This attitude is recorded in an extensive oral history of the Carter White House based on the testimony of 70 administrators interviewed at the Miller Center.
13. Kenneth W. Thompson, *Winston S. Churchill: Statesmenship and Power* (Baton Rouge, Louisiana: Louisiana State University Press, 1983).
14. Kenneth W. Thompson, editor, *The American Presidency: Principles and Problems,* Volume II (Washington, D.C.: University Press of America, 1983).

PART THREE

Theorists and Policymakers
In the Cold War

The Cold War: Morgenthau's Approach

The Cold War is the great drama of the twentieth century. In a sense it is much closer to the human drama than hot war, for it is more filled with pathos and contradictions, persisting problems and conflicting values; it reflects the need of learning to live with adversity. Full-scale war pits nations in arms against one another; it organizes a people who are ideologically united. It has its roots in the *levée en masse,* in thoroughgoing national unity. It is a post-revolutionary phenomenon wherein all the less-than-national differences are subsumed within a common purpose; the national will is focused against a common enemy. A nation in war purges society of conflicts and differences and unifies north and south, black and white, capitalists and socialists within the national boundaries. This is the reason veterans look back nostalgically to the wartime days of camaraderie and mutual trust. Limited war or cold war arouses far fewer such emotions and, if they appear, fails to sustain them.

1. THE COLD WAR AS HUMAN CONDITION

National and international politics cannot be equated with war although the prospect of war is inescapably bound up with world politics. The human condition is one of ambiguity, disputes over means and ends, actions and overreactions. The struggle for identity and recognition is endlessly pursued. In world politics, myths and common purpose are not one but many. Misunderstandings and misconceptions divide men and nations. There are few operative sources of unifying purpose and agreed-upon ends among

93

nations. Historically, wars, like athletic contests, tend to be measured and charted by victory or defeat. Politics and the Cold War
can seldom be measured in that way nor the course of our daily
lives. "Life is one problem after another," observed the harried
housewife. Walt Whitman put it more elegantly:

> It is provided in the very essence of things that from any
> fruition of success, no matter what, shall come forth
> something to make a greater struggle necessary.

Yet mankind from the Creation has resisted this truth. If life
has its persistent problems, someone else is to blame. For Adam it
was "the woman" who gave him the apple to eat. For contemporaries,
it is "the system." The one fact men most stubbornly resist and
seek to refute by dogmas and myths is the ubiquity of problems;
acceptance of problems is anathema to the dynamics of life itself.
The twin sources of a healthy human existence, evidently, are,
first, a sense of movement ("going someplace") and, second, a
haven from pain and problems, an end to all struggles and conflicts.
Religiously, these are expressed in the biblical phrase "We cannot
rest until we rest in thee," by the New Jerusalem and the Promised
Land, and in secular terms by utopias, the "good" or the "new"
society and the "heavenly city." Americans in particular are
perplexed, bewildered, and angered by those who speak of ceaseless troubles and unending problems. Senator Abraham Ribicoff in
his second congressional campaign set forth in utter candor the
issues that neither he nor others had solved or were likely to solve.
In this campaign, he suffered the one defeat of his political career.
President Lincoln's anguished inner struggles led some to doubt his
sanity, and Adlai Stevenson's torment and despair cast him in the
image of an indecisive man whom the people twice rejected in
presidential campaigns. Secretary General Dag Hammarskjold's
counsel at the start of difficult negotiations, "Gentlemen, we must
advance to the status quo ante," ran counter to every prevailing idea
of progress, and to the end of his life Hammarskjold was portrayed
as a mystic. The notion of holding one's own, of buying time or
making the best of a bad situation, is alien to the American psyche.

Carried to extremes, reconciling oneself to inevitable problems
may become a sign of alienation and dis-ease (the etymology of
disease suggests that sound health is bound up with a sense of
untroubled ease). Dis-ease can lead to crippling indecision (Hamlet),

to withdrawal from reality (the youth caught between conflicting loyalties to warring parents retreating and closing the doors of his room), to passivity in politics (*ohne mich*—without me—in German politics), to schizophrenia (becoming two persons and living alternately in two worlds) or paranoia (explaining one's troubles exclusively in terms of personal or national devils). Studies by psychologists of the restless suburban housewife show that escape from boredom for some community-minded women means finding rational alternatives (such as joining the League of Women Voters) or irrational ones (such as indulging in buying sprees or extramarital adventures), ways out of a life overcome by emptiness, hopelessness, and despair. The line is admittedly a fine one between falling prey to dis-eased states of mind and learning to live with excrutiatingly difficult and seemingly insoluble problems. There are limits to human endurance. A period of ceaseless and unremitting problems, a succession of difficulties for which there seems no answer, a prolonged "winter of discontent," is probably more than anyone can bear.

Everyone needs a feeling of going somewhere and accomplishing something. The most pitiful example of a sense of hopelessness and of no place to go may be the American nursing home (for some the American prison is the scene of utter despair). The better nursing home administrators tell us that the most-needed therapy to counter hopelessness is finding a way of bringing those patients back from the retreat from life to a renewed sense of participation and involvement. The rewards of the active as compared with the contemplative life are a sense of accomplishment and movement—a reaffirmation of life over death. Not by accident the infantry soldier is taught and drilled to know that survival depends on movement; the command of the infantry platoon leader is "Follow me," and for the foot soldier "Don't just stand there, do something" is the first law. To be immobilized or pinned down by enemy fire comes to be equated with death. Even in scholarship, for many it is more liberating to write or find other outlets in self-expression than it is to carry out the hard, grubby, often painful acts of study and research. It is easier somehow to combine teaching and learning or writing and learning than learning as an end in itself. In George Kennan's words, true scholarship demands a form of monastic life, but this requires inner resources and strength which few present-day scholars possess.

If all this were the solitary individual's problem, it might be worth a footnote, but hardly a lengthy disquisition. It takes us, however, curiously enough direct to the heart of the nation's problem (and that of other nations as well) in confronting the Cold War. The conflict calls for qualities of mind not always displayed by Americans. Practically every thoughtful observer from the birth of the Republic to the present has described Americans as a dynamic, ebullient, and optimistic people determined and able to solve problems which had been the scourge of mankind from the beginning of history.

Optimism and hope were the wellsprings of early greatness and in the colonial era permeated national life. In *Letters from an American Farmer,* Crèvecoeur could write of the new society:

> We have no princes, for whom we toil, starve, and bleed:
> we are the most perfect society now existing in the world.
> Here man is free as he ought to be, nor is this pleasing
> equality so transitory as many others are.[1]

On the question of poverty and equality, the more restrained Benjamin Franklin was to say, "The truth is that there are in this . . . country few people so miserable as the poor of Europe." It mattered little that such expressions hid or obscured the distinctions between free men and slaves, or elites of talent or property. What gave these proclamations credibility was the belief that history was being transformed, that here was a land in which there were neither permanent rulers nor permanent subjects. The founders of the Republic had little doubt they had reached a new heaven and new earth. Not only was there work to be done and progress which lay ahead but the end of the process was embodied in the beginning. Thomas Jefferson proclaimed this in a letter to John Adams on natural aristocracy, October 28, 1813: "Before the establishment of the American States, nothing was known to history but the man of the old world crowded within limits either small or overcharged, and steeped in vices which the situation generates."[2] What mattered most was that these affirmations seemed confirmed by early American history. The frontier and, later, superior technology provided an outlet for the adventurous and ambitious. The fortuitous coincidence of geographic isolation and the European balance of power freed the fledgling nation from the burdens and complexities of international responsibility.

In such a world, it was tempting to assume that a new and less troubled stage in history had been reached and that progress was foreordained and assured. The end then was seen in the beginning, and hope and optimism were firmly grounded in the utopia already attained.

2. THE NATURE OF THE COLD WAR

The movement from this way of thinking to the present is a journey into another world. The era of the Cold War is one in which both the end of the road and the journey are shrouded in doubt, imponderables, and uncertainty. The most urgent goal is negative, not positive — "to prevent the thermonuclear destruction of the world." For the first time in history, a generation has been born and is living out its days under an ominous mushrooming cloud which could mean the destruction of the world. Presidents and secretaries of state, whatever they have said along the way, point with pride, in leaving office, not to having built a new society, established a world of law, or triumphed over adversaries, but to having staved off mutual annihilation, thus preserving an old society. The more they know, the more they are possessed by the threat to mankind's survival. It is this threat that makes the Cold War unique and requires a new mind set, a new philosophy of international relations, and a body of new precepts and doctrines.

Despite all this, the vocabulary and rhetoric of international politics have remained essentially the same, and the gulf between the private and public language of statesmen has grown even deeper. In public, leaders speak of triumphing over bolshevism, liberating eastern Europe, rolling back communism, defending freedom everywhere, and ending the Cold War. In private, they proceed from the balance of terror, probe for mutually acceptable areas of arms control, recognize limitations and constraints, cooperate with Communists when in the national interest, and even accept — detestable words — worldwide spheres of interest. The stages on which the dramas of world politics are performed are novel, but the motives and tactics of nations are not much different from what they have ever been. Nations put national security first, proceed on the basis of national interests, use diplomatic machinery to serve their own ends—not the world's ends, whatever they may be. They act or desist from acting in world politics more often from ambition and fear then from devotion to any global ideological design. They have permanent interests but no permanent friends. If this were not so, an American president who had been among the twentieth century's most outspoken foes of worldwide Communism would not have fashioned a policy of rapprochement with the most populous of all Communist countries. If it were not so, the twentieth century's most ruthless Communist leader, Stalin, would not have favored the China of Chiang Kai-shek over that of Mao Tse-tung until the eleventh hour, or held back support of independent Communist parties in Europe. President Nixon and Premier Stalin in their policies put American and Russian national interest first while continuing to speak the ideological language of democracy and Communism. And when the Vietnam War came to an end and the United States withdrew its power, signals went up from another Communist country, North Vietnam, appealing to the United States to preserve a limited presence as a balancing force against the expanding influence of Russia and China—its partners in the Communist world.

The paradox of the Cold War, then, is that its rhetoric is the language of war: victory and defeat, good and evil, utopia and antiutopia, black and white. Cold War policy, by contrast, is determined by *Realpolitik,* advance and retreat, testing and probing, and salvage operations, all of which fall in the gray area of partial gains and losses, limited advances and retreats, and the balancing of power. In all this there is little which is new in the annals of statecraft. What is new is that absolute power in the hands of the two superstates, too lethal and terrifying to contemplate, has rendered them powerless to seize the historic fruits of power. Yet neither is willing or able to acknowledge these limits openly to its public. The ultimate contradiction, therefore, is that the language of the Cold War bears scant relationship to the conduct of that war.

Curiously, this idea of limits, of constraints and of human fallibility, is accepted and understood in man's workaday world and taken in stride everywhere as a guide to conduct. Surely this is true in the family. Parents learn early the truth of Reinhold Niebuhr's wise comment: "The most one can hope is that he do as little harm as possible to his children." Only the pathos experienced directly in parenthood can convey the full weight of this truth and the iron law that the interests of the parent and the child are not the same at any given time, and cannot be, if either is to realize true identity. The Indonesian cultural historian, Soedjatmoko, a trustee of the Ford Foundation and perhaps Asia's most profound student of international relations, has asked in how many instances husband and wife in a lifetime of living together truly perceive and understand one another's deepest values and feelings. To most of them genuine mutual understanding is denied to the very end of their lives. Much of human existence is a tragic story of missed opportunities, a misreading of another's motives, a failure to perceive intentions, a vast network of misconceptions and misunderstandings. And the more the whole process becomes frozen in hard and inflexible doctrines and stereotypes, the less likely are the prospects for breakthroughs to new levels of understanding. The ancients were more at home with this truth, as exemplified in Marcus Aurelius's words: "Our understandings are always liable to error. Nature and certainty are very hard to come at, and infallibility is mere vanity and pretence."

What is true in the most intimate of human relations cannot help but be true amid the perplexities of all the shifting patterns and political alignments of great collectivities. The Cold War, at one level, represents the clash of two competing world systems bent on shaping if not imposing social and political doctrines. At another level, it is a struggle—forecast by nineteenth-century political prophets as diverse as Napoleon and Alexis de Tocqueville and by many others—of two emerging great powers destined to become the dominant forces of mid-twentieth-century international politics. In Alexis de Tocqueville's words:

> There are on the earth today two great peoples, who, from different points of departure, seem to be advancing toward the same end. They are the Russians and the Anglo-Americans. Both have grown in obscurity, and while the attention of mankind was occupied elsewhere they have suddenly taken their places in the first rank among the nations, and the world has learned, almost at the same time, both of their birth and of their greatness.
>
> Their points of departure are different, their paths are divergent; nevertheless, each seems summoned by a secret

design of providence to hold in his hands, some day, the destinies of half the world.[3]

What Tocqueville, writing in the 1830s, perceived as historical inevitability is one dimension of the Cold War—a dimension frequently neglected by the ideologues of protracted conflict. It was the objective situation and historic Russian and American behavior that led to conflict and rivalry—a contest which would have occurred even if Karl Marx had never written the *Communist Manifesto*. The two countries were destined to confront one another as competing centers of power had done throughout the history of the European state system. The clash of massive Russian and American concentrations of power was no accident of history but a necessary and predictable result of forces beyond the control of individuals and ideologies. In Louis Halle's words, men see "their future in their present as one sees the leaf in the bud."[4] What in fact came to pass would have come to pass regardless of the ideological label attached to the authoritarian regime that governed Russia.

For Halle and a small but growing number of historians, the role of Communism, therefore, is secondary in the polarization of the world:

> What the Revolution of 1917 did was simply to reinvigorate the traditional principle of authoritarianism in Russia. It replaced a decadent and enfeebled authoritarian dynasty with a new, vigorous, and ruthlessly determined authoritarian dynasty. . . . The Cold War, then, represents an historical necessity to which the communist movement is incidental rather than essential.[5]

For other historians, including those who substantially agree with Halle's analysis, this is only part of the story, albeit a large and neglected chapter. It was Hans J. Morgenthau's view that if there had been nothing more to the conflict than a great power struggle between the Soviet Union and the West,

> in all likelihood, that conflict would not have issued in a cold war, but would have petered out, as did the conflict following World War I. . . . The new dimension which set this conflict apart from its predecessor and transformed it into a cold war was the communist character of the

Soviet state and of its foreign policy. More particularly, it was Stalin's fusion of the traditional national interests of Russia with the tenets of communism and its misunderstanding by the West, as well as Stalin's misunderstanding of the West's reaction that were responsible for that transformation.[6]

Summing up his conclusions on the origins of the Cold War, Morgenthau wrote:

> To have transformed the tenets of communism into instruments for Russia's traditional foreign policy was the great innovative contribution Stalin made to the foreign policy of the Soviet Union. The nature of this contribution has been widely misunderstood. The Western world has looked upon Stalin as an orthodox Bolshevik, the fanatical proponent of a "rigid theology" [Arthur Schlesinger, Jr.'s phrase] bent upon spreading the communist gospel indiscriminately and by hook or crook to the four corners of the earth. Those who hold this view judge Stalin as though he were Trotsky: they confound Stalin's means which comprise the classic communist methods, ruthlessly applied, with his ends, which were in the tradition of Czarist expansionism rather than of Marxist-Leninist promotion of world revolution as an end in itself. Actually, in relation to Marxism-Leninism, Stalin's foreign policy was distinct from Lenin's and Trotsky's, on the one hand, and from that of Khrushchev and his successors, on the other.[7]

For Morgenthau, as for Halle, the primary determinant of Soviet advance was Russian imperialism. At the same time, he saw Communism as a dynamic and empowering force unique in Russian history. He was absorbed in studying the relation between the two and tracing the pattern from one stage to the next in Soviet foreign policy. Understanding the Cold War for him meant understanding this relationship.

Because Morgenthau had both a clear conception of the nature of man and the historian's sense of what is unique and recurrent, he approached Soviet-American relations from a perspective which continues to have enduring value. It would be difficult to think of any contemporary thinker whose legacy of writings on the Cold

War match Morgenthau's vision. In part, the consistency of his thought resulted from his insistence that Western policymakers must be guided by a sound understanding of the nature of the threat in the Cold War. He warned of the " . . . confusion which does not see that the real issue is Russian imperialism and Communist revolution only insofar as it is an instrument of that imperialism."[8] He called on the historical parallel of the Napoleonic Wars when Britain had faced a revolutionary challenge. Britain's wisest statesmen, in formulating foreign policy, had concluded that: "Revolutions that adversely affected the national interests of Britain were to be opposed. There was neither the need to oppose all revolution indiscriminately, nor the power to do so successfully."[9] Yet in the early stages of the Cold War, it was indiscriminate opposition against the expansion of Communism everywhere that became the dominant creed. The schism that grew up between two Communist states, the Soviet Union and China, should have led observers to question the universalistic doctrine that in American foreign policy direct opposition to Communism everywhere was both necessary and possible. The credibility of indiscriminate anti-Communism as the basis of foreign policy has survived down to the present because it provides a simple explanation of all the world's problems. More important, it holds out the promise to Americans that once Communism is defeated and destroyed, a trouble-free world will be possible once more. (The residual faith of Americans in secular utopias survives.)

Fifteen years after Morgenthau's warnings against the illusions of indiscriminate anti-Communism at the outset of the Cold War, he again challenged a policy which was justified in the name of anti-Communism and patriotism. He maintained that no one could demonstrate that vital American interests were engaged in Vietnam. Secretary Dulles had defended the first cautious and provisional American involvement in Vietnam by arguing that the United States should undertake to salvage certain historic Western interests after the French left Vietnam. Dulles knew better than to believe that foreign policy could be conducted as a worldwide crusade against an alien ideology. In an essay written before the Cold War, he had explained:

> Practical political action is not often a subject for authoritative moral judgments of universal scope. Those who act

in the political field must deal with the possible, not with the ideal; they must try to get the relatively good, the lesser evil; they cannot without frustration reject whatever is not wholly good; they cannot be satisfied with proclaimed ends but must deal with actual means.[10]

For domestic and international political reasons, Dulles abandoned his own precepts of foreign policy and justified intervention by saying that Communism had to be resisted on the ground wherever it threatened or it would spread. Tragically, it was the legacy of the Cold War Dulles and not that of Dulles writing before the Cold War that guided his successors and led on to setbacks in the struggle.

In the 1960s, Morgenthau, now in his mid-sixties, summoned all his energies to oppose this viewpoint. If indiscriminate anti-Communism had any basis as a basis for American foreign policy it was in the 1940s and 1950s when Russian imperialism and Soviet Communism were the dominant threat. By the late 1950s, new forces appeared

with a variety of communisms, whose relations with the Soviet Union and China change from country to country and from time to time and whose bearing upon the interests of the United States requires empirical examination in each instance.... The bearing which the pursuit of these interests has upon the policies of the United States must be determined, in terms not of communist ideology, but of their compatibility with the interests of the United States.[11]

For Morgenthau, the operative principle was that intervention had to rest on something more specific than antiCommunism. "Intervene we must when our national interest requires it and when our power gives us a chance to succeed."[12] When America's vital interests were threatened in Europe or Asia by the expansion of the Soviet Union or China, the United States would have no choice. It had to seek ways of containing its rivals, and they should have no reason to doubt our intentions. However, a mere Communist presence anywhere in the world, however distasteful, was not enough to engage American interests. American intervention was justified when our foreign policy objectives and interests required it.

What Morgenthau opposed was the assumption that communism everywhere in the world is not only morally unacceptable and philosophically hostile to the United States, but also detrimental to the national interests of the United States and therefore must be opposed on political and military as well as on moral and philosophical grounds. . . . This provided a justification for the United States to intervene not only against Communist takeovers, but against all radical revolutionary movements, lest they be taken over by the Communists.[13]

3. THE MORGENTHAU LEGACY IN UNPUBLISHED WRITINGS

Morgenthau was consistent in formulating his view of the Cold War throughout the last decade of an enormously productive career. Time and again, he spoke out against the militarization of the Cold War partly because he understood that the nature of the struggle was more than a military conflict and partly because he knew that a military resolution of the conflict was impossible without universal destruction given the realities of the nuclear age. Moreover, he grasped, at a level of understanding which escaped many of his contemporaries, the impossibility of solving all the world's troubles through American political and military intervention. He was skeptical of the intent and possibilities of the human rights campaign of the Carter administration. Having learned to live with ambiguity in his personal life, he could not accept the illusion that ideal societies were possible around the world by American fiat. He understood that the possibility of transforming the world which was the goal of some Carter spokesmen coincided in time with what he called "The Contraction of America." He was convinced that the contraction was not a temporary phenomenon brought about by events such as the Civil War or an economic crisis but was a permanent reality. "On the world stage, there is no place into which the United States could expand without risking either nuclear war, as in the Cuban missile crisis of 1962, or at best stalemate, if not defeat, as in Indochina."[14] He believed that the moral self-identification which had reenforced the hope of Americans and attracted the rest of the world had "suffered a terrible blow through the Indochina war and Watergate." He was fearful of how Americans would respond to the new reality, facing up to the necessity of "redefining American identity and mission" or making "a futile, and perhaps fatal, effort at superimposing an obsolete consciousness of expansion upon a recalcitrant reality of contraction." Whoever witnessed the first presidential term of the Reagan administration cannot be reassured that his fears even now are groundless.

Morgenthau's worries about the militarization of the Cold War and too great a dependence on client states whom we sought to make militarily strong came to a head in his unpublished writings concerning growing instability in the Middle East. Here too the consistency of his thought is apparent. The fall of the Shah and the failure of the United States to support him confirmed his doubts that military alliances with one or more supposed bastions of strength could safeguard American interests. He had written critically of Secretary Dulles's policy of pactomania in the 1950s. In opposing arms sales of highly sophisticated aircraft to Saudi Arabia, Morgenthau reflected his concern for the security of Israel, a concern which grew even stronger in the last years of his life. His critics hastened to point out that his pro-Israel commitment rather than his political realism prompted his recommendations for the area. Yet there is more to his position than his critics have acknowledged. With Kissinger, Morgenthau believed that peace was the highest moral value in a competing hierarchy of moral values. He wrote that the new "aircraft in Saudi Arabian hands would constitute a new and serious threat to Israel and, conversely, to Saudi Arabia. The very existence of such mutual threats would increase the risks of war."[15]

Thus Morgenthau in the final statements constituting his legacy in the Cold War returned to the point at which he had begun. He was unchanging in his position that the Cold War would not be settled through arms alone, although he recognized the importance of strength and containment and called in his last years for increasing military preparedness. The continued introduction of arms into Asia and the Middle East increased the possibility of conflict. No one can say for sure what his judgment might have been of Israel's bombing of Iraq's nuclear installation or invasion of Lebanon. Two of his oft-repeated principles would have been in tension and conflict. All through the Carter administration, he questioned the indiscriminate nonproliferation policy of that administration. He asked how the United States could long deny to Brazil, India, or Pakistan the same right to build nuclear defenses which it had claimed for itself. At the same time, he fervently defended Israel's right to provide for its own national security. One thing is sure: his analysis would have been more complex and many-sided than the judgments of either all-out apologists or critics of Israel.

In the last year of his life, he grew increasingly anxious about a Middle East conflict that would spread and erupt into a global conflict. It was the merging of regional and greatpower rivalry in the area that filled him with alarm. His loyalty to Israel was unquestioned, but his devotion to the survival of mankind was even stronger. He often remarked, "Death is an absurdity," and, despite his focus on the national interest, he extended his concern for the individual to the whole human race. He was more troubled about the Soviet intervention in Afghanistan than many of his liberal friends. While he was not unmindful of the historical contingencies that prompted the intervention, he feared it symbolized a new adventurism and recklessness on the part of Soviet leaders and a shift in the balance of forces within the Politburo.

He talked in my last extended conversation with him of the possibility of Soviet movement from the north to the Persian Gulf. The true challenge in the region was Soviet intervention, not the Arab-Israeli dispute. In the Middle East as in every other world region, he warned that nuclear conflict might occur as a result of accident. Neither side, he believed, wanted war, but war might come and in a nuclear war the victors would be indistinguishable from the victims. War between the superpowers could not be a war for national objectives. Instead, it would be a conflict of mutual annihilation. In the end, what had transformed the Cold War was neither traditional great-power rivalry nor the contest between conflicting political ideologies. It was the reality of nuclear weapons.

If Morgenthau was right in his analysis of nuclear war, his legacy of living with all the contradictions and ambiguities of the Cold War may be more enduring than any of us at first supposed. For his political realism, linking power conflicts with diplomatic accommodation, may not only be the best of possible alternative approaches to the Cold War. It may be the only viable and workable approach if mankind is to survive.[16]

NOTES

1. J. Hector St. John Crèvecosur, *Letters from an American Farmer* (New York: Dutton, 1912), pp. 40–41.
2. Thomas Jefferson, *The Writings of Thomas Jefferson,* edited by Albert E. Bergh, 20 vols. (Washington, 1907), 13: 401.
3. Alexis de Tocqueville, *Democracy in America,* quoted in Louis J. Halle, *The Cold War as History* (London: Chatto & Windus, 1967), p. 10.
4. *Ibid.,* p. 11.
5. *Ibid.,* pp. 11–12.
6. Lloyd C. Gardner, Arthur Schlesinger, Jr., and Hans J. Morgenthau, *The Origins of the Cold War* (Waltham, Mass.: Ginn, 1976), p. 92.
7. *Ibid.,* pp. 92–93.
8. Hans J. Morgenthau, *In Defense of the National Interest* (New York: Knopf, 1951), p. 80.
9. *Ibid.,* p. 86.
10. John Foster Dulles, "The Church and International Disorder," quoted in Townsend Hoopes, *The Devil and John Foster Dulles* (Boston: Little, Brown, 1973), p. 118.
11. Hans J. Morgenthau, *A New Foreign Policy for the United States* (New York: Praeger, 1969), p. 126.
12. *Ibid.,* p. 128.
13. *Ibid.,* pp. 124–125.
14. Hans J. Morgenthau, "The Contraction of America," unpublished manuscript, p. 2.
15. Hans J. Morgenthau, unpublished essay on arms sales, p. 4.
16. A slightly different version of this chapter appeared in *Social Research,* Vol. 48, No. 4.

Churchill and the Cold War

On the eve of World War II, Winston S. Churchill wrote: "The modern world presents the extraordinary spectacle of almost everybody wishing to prevent or avoid war, and yet war coming remorselessly nearer to almost everybody. Surely this will be the great mystery which future generations will find among the records, and perhaps the ruins of our age." Historians will ask themselves how western societies comprised of vast numbers of well educated and for the most part virtuous men and women fell victim to the grim perils of war. The answer according to Churchill will be: "They had no plan."

Strikingly enough, Churchill's terse statement of what is required to stop war is as timely today as it was in the years before World War II. It is puzzling why leaders who came after him, including present day chief executives, have shied away from his prescriptions for peace. The fact that Churchill spoke with such clarity on the prerequisites for the maintenance of peace justifies his inclusion in a volume on moralism and morality largely related to leadership and institutions. Because he held to a fairly consistent line of thought on foreign policy, his philosophy may serve as an example for others including American presidents.

For Americans in the postwar era, it has become fashionable to say that peace depends on the United Nations or international law or resisting aggression and to pursue these worthy objectives as ends in themselves. Alternatively, other leaders have maintained that pragmatism offered the best guide to foreign policy. In the absence of a plan, Western leaders have proceeded case by case out of a conviction that each successive crisis was unique. Yet in the final analysis, modern leaders have grounded their policies on hidden assumptions and inarticulated premises. They have proceeded on the basis of largely unexamined propositions. Thus some have said the sole determinant of successful foreign policy was strength and have made military preparedness the only guiding principle of policy. Being number one as a world military power has become the supreme goal for the nation without asking "number one for what?" Others have proposed the negotiation of universal disarmament and, failing that, some form of unilateral disarmament without examining the consequences for national security. If it is true, as Lord Franks has argued, that "the most prevalent single cause of misunderstanding and suspicion . . . [is] failure to communicate the assumptions of a proposal" then critical comparison of these views is essential.

Churchill's importance in twentieth century statescraft, especially before and after World War II, results from the twin pillars on which he sought to base foreign policy: strength and negotiations. From 1936 to 1939, he wrote fortnightly letters commenting primarily on issues of foreign policy. He set forth his views in the most simple and straightforward language. No plan, he wrote, had any value unless it had behind it force and the resolve to use force. Imperialism would not be turned back without a Grand Alliance founded on the combined efforts of nations threatened by such imperialism, whether the threat was Philip of Macedonia setting out to conquer the Greek city-states or Napoleon and Hitler overrunning Europe. Peace must have its constables; the scales of justice have no influence lacking the sword. Not only one nation confronting an aggressor but all nations whose security is jeopardized must join together. However, history demonstrates that the counsel of united strength, so obviously sound in the abstract, has gone largely unheeded. Nations who faced a common threat have been lulled into believing they could escape the sacrifices required by a common defense effort; they have sought security by making a deal, retreating into isolation or relying on their own strength.

While Churchill understood the essential nature of the common defense, he also recognized the different perspectives from which nations viewed the threat to peace. The aggressor appeared in different forms to different countries. For some the danger was near, for others less immediate and for still others far off. Theorists of collective security maintained that peace was indivisible and each nation should join every other: "who touches one, touches all." To demand that nations act without regard for their particular interests, however, was to ask more than mankind at its present stage of development could sustain.

Therefore, in giving content to his plan for strength, Churchill called for zones of responsibility and regional structures. He wrote: "In the front line, pledged to all the necessary measures, well-equipped, strictly combined, stand those who dwell nearest to the Potential Aggressor; in the second line those likely to be next affected, or indirectly affected, by his aggression. Farther off, and least heavily committed, will be the states who, while they do not fear this particular Potential Aggressor, nevertheless realize that some day . . . their turn may come." It would be divorcing practice from reality to expect nations in the three zones to respond to each successive threat as if it touched them equally and in the same way. To weave together the varied regional and national interests into one worldwide organism, Churchill maintained, recognizing that the engagement of each nation must fit the occasion, was the inexorable task of world statesmen. If some states were by virtue of their interests and power destined to take the lead, others according to their respective interests and power must band together. The alternative was to be destroyed one by one. In Churchill's words: " . . . a series of regional pacts included in a Grand Alliance or League offers . . . the sole hope of preventing war or of preventing, if war should come, the ruin of those who have done no wrong."

Churchill's plan for peace in contrast with those of a multitude of contemporary leaders was not exhausted in his appeal for strength. It rested as well on a strategy of diplomacy. What he offered the world was a framework for considering the relationship between strength and diplomacy, between power and negotiations. No one is more deserving of the title "defender of freedom," Churchill stands supreme as the father of the doctrine that security depends on strength, that the appetite of an aggressor feeds on success. Often forgotten, however, is the fact that in perhaps his most famous speech at Fulton, Missouri, rallying the West to the defense of freedom against Soviet expansionism, he also declared: "What is needed is a settlement, and the longer it is delayed, the more difficult it will be and the greater our dangers will become." On December 10, 1948, Churchill addressed the House of Commons saying: "I have frequently advised that we should endeavour to reach a settlement with Russia on fundamentally outstanding questions. . . . I believe that in this resides the best hope of avoiding a third world war." On December 14, 1950, he dealt specifically with the view that negotiations meant appeasement: "The declaration of the Prime Minister that there will be no appeasement ... commands almost universal support. It is a good slogan for the country. It seems to me, however, that ... it requires to be more precisely defined." Churchill, then leader of the opposition, went on to explain: "What we really mean, I think, is no appeasement through weakness or fear." It was weakness not strength that led Chamberlain into appeasement at Munich and Churchill came to office to rectify that error. But in 1950, he linked strength with diplomacy saying: "Appeasement in itself may be good or bad according to circumstances. Appeasement from weakness and fear is alike futile and fatal. Appeasement from strength is magnanimous and noble and might be the surest and perhaps the only path to peace."

Churchill's plan for peace constituted a doctrine or an organizing theory of foreign policy. He was persuaded that no leader could deal with the contingencies of world politics without such a theory. In his words: "Those who are possessed of a definite body of doctrine and of deeply rooted convictions upon it will be in a much better position to deal with the shifts and surprises of daily affairs." In this sense, the "right" political decision is the outcome of a powerful and creative mind possessed of a body of doctrine comprehending the varied dimensions of a given political situation. Wisdom involves an evaluation of the intractable elements in a complex situation. Clarity of vision depends on a scaffolding of thought that includes certain bedrock principles concerning man, politics and society. To paraphrase the poet, T. S. Eliot, without a philosophy or a plan, wisdom will be lost in knowledge and knowledge in information.

Churchill's philosophy and thought grounded in certain historic views of man and politics represents a counter force to the prevailing trends of the times. Contemporary culture is endlessly tempted to cope with its problems by piling facts on facts. The age is the era of the computer. Statistics are more complete and we have more accurate records of birth rates, death rates and emigration rates. Elemental factors responsible for the growth and prosperity of nations are better understood and more subject to control. Yet while knowledge has increased, so have the factors that must be identified and evaluated. In place of once isolated rivalries, we face struggles that involve directly or indirectly the whole habitable globe. Our problems have become so vast and interconnected, their solution so painful and doubtful, and the weight of contingencies so overwhelming that wise statesmen are needed as never before.

Withal, the essential character of problems in international politics is not new. However much we speak of change, men and states have confronted one another in the past across vast expanses of geography embracing values and interests that persist for generations. The continuity of foreign policies is a reality because national interests in broad outline persist and the suspicion of state for state has survived. Political movements that are alive only to change not continuity flounder in the international arena. Writing of his own Labor Party, Denis Healey could write: "Because the Party as a whole lacks any systematic theory of world affairs, it has too often fallen victim to the besetting sin of all progressive movements—utopianism. In particular it tends to discount the power elements in politics, seeing it as a specific evil of the existing system rather than a generic characteristic of politics as such."

Churchill approached foreign policy in terms of power and diplomacy. For the most part, he resisted the temptation to set aside his doctrine in practice. In a debate in the House of Commons he declared: "Foreign policy is not a game, nor is it an academic question, and . . . not an ideological question. . . . Foreign policy is in fact a method of protecting our own interests and saving our own people from the threat of another war, and it is against that criterion that the foreign policy of any government is to be measured." A doctrine provides guidelines but the statesman must be flexible in its application. It can be said of foreign policy as Churchill wrote of warfare: "the best plan of acquiring flexibility is to have three or four plans for all the possible contingencies, all worked out with the utmost detail. Then it is much easier to switch from one to the other as and where the cat jumps." With flexibility, the leader is not shackled; the doctrine is not a straightjacket. The alternatives are never ideal cases for applying a principle, and they conflict with one another in various ways. In one context, the Soviet Union is the threat, but, confronted by Hitler's Germany, Churchill declared bluntly he would make a pact with the devil to stop Germany's expansion. On October 18, 1951, Churchill defended Britain's policy in the Middle East against its critics: "Our own self-interest demands that we take cognizance of the Muslim world, its legitimate aspirations, and try to help out."

Churchill's firm grasp of world politics was rooted in history. His conception of the Grand Alliance was based on the lessons of the coalition that resisted Louis XIV. His historical masterpiece, *Marlborough: His Life and Times,* was written during the decade of "The Gathering Storm," about which he warned not *ex post facto* but as the first signs of dark clouds appeared on the horizon. Marlborough was the linchpin of the first Grand Alliance that thwarted France's attempt to dominate Europe, so Churchill led in marshalling the resistance to German expansionism and again at Fulton, Missouri, in calling for unity to oppose Soviet expansion. Yet resistance was not an end in itself. By the 1950s, Churchill on no less than forty occasions had called for an approach to the Russians in the quest for a peaceful settlement. Fifteen months after the Fulton Speech he declared before Parliament: "It is idle to reason or argue with the Communists. It is, however, possible to deal with them on a fair, realistic basis, and, in my experience, they will keep their bargains as long as it is in their interest to do so, which might, in this grave matter, be a long time, once things were settled."

Churchill's plan was not always followed and, when followed by his successors, was not always applied with the same wisdom and skill he might have employed. Because he had a plan based on twin pillars of peace, he pursued a steady course. For that reason, Churchill's philosophy can provide lessons for American presidents as well as for military policymakers and diplomats. His life and works provide a handbook for contemporary leaders who search for an interconnection between defense and diplomacy. For this reason, Churchill remains the consummate example of the leader who combines theory and practice. He was both historian and policymaker. He sought to learn from the past as he fashioned a vision of the future. His view of the Cold War has enduring value as is true of few past or present policymakers.

PART FOUR

Moralism, Morality and The Nuclear Question

Power, Force and Diplomacy

The present crisis has generated intense debate over the instruments of foreign policy the United States has at its disposal and controversy over their use in particular stages of a dispute or conflict. The debate has centered over the meaning and use of power and force. A little more than a decade ago, writing *On Violence* in an era when its primary manifestation was within national boundaries, the American political philosopher, the late Hannah Arendt, sought to distinguish between violence and power, saying: " . . . power always stands in need of numbers, whereas violence up to a point . . . relies on implements."[1] Writers differ on concepts such as power and violence. Power for some is conceived as the ability of the individual or the group to impose its will on others. Power for Arendt implied the human ability to act in concert—*potestas in populo;* without a people or group there is no power in politics. Power for individuals and groups is linked with prestige and authority. In politics, authority requires respect either for a person or an office; its enemy is contempt or laughter directed at the person or office. In both foreign relations and domestic affairs, "violence appears as a last resort to keep . . . power . . . intact against individual challengers—the foreign enemy, the native criminal. . . . " or to overthrow authority.[2] It would seem, therefore, that force and violence are the prerequisites of power and power nothing but a facade. In a violent world, it is force that counts not power which is dependent on force.

Yet, political events such as revolutions teach that the exact opposite is true, for everything depends on the power behind force and violence. "The sudden dramatic breakdown of power that ushers in revolution reveals in a flash how civil obedience—to laws, to rulers, to institutions—is but the outward manifestation of support and consent."[3] This leads to the conclusion that: "power and violence are opposites; where the one rules absolutely the other is absent. . . . Violence can destroy power; it is utterly incapable of creating it."[4] Where a nation has commanding political power, force and violence need not come in to play. This principle underlies the strategy of deterrence in a nuclear age.

Mankind's predicament in international politics is that, particularly in periods of tumultous change, all forms of power and international authority are in question. Rebellious states reserve "contempt and laughter" for both the person (Mr. Waldheim or Mr. Cuellar) and the office (the Secretary General of the United Nations or the Judges of the World Court) of international authorities which are either lacking in power or associated with an unjust or unfriendly status quo. When international authority proves ineffective, powerful states intervene and confront the weak; historically in such confrontations the powerful have prevailed. In recent times, however, the powerful despite their power have been seen to be powerless. The consequences of the employment of power capable of destroying civilization have reduced the power of the mightiest states in limited conflict. Further, their acting effectively and sometimes in concert has been rendered difficult if not impossible by the breakdown of moral and political consensus particularly between the United States and the USSR.

The effective exercise of power by states internationally has throughout history been dependent on three sources only partly associated with force: expectation of benefits, fear of disadvantages, and respect for men and institutions. Respect for Roman law and British political institutions helped to strengthen their power in the world. For societies including international society in transition, respect is held in suspense. In its place, men and nations in their psychological relations seek to influence one another through holding out possible benefits or threatening actions that will cause disadvantage to others. The prestige of a nation or a leader is an intangible element of political power independent of the actual use of force. Whatever the material or military objectives of a nation's foreign policy, ultimately it seeks to control the actions of others through influence over their minds even when it has recourse to the use of force. It has been said that: "The political objective of war itself is not *per se* the conquest of territory or the annihilation of enemy armies, but a change in the mind of the enemy which will make him yield to the will of the victor."[5]

Yet, inasmuch as war remains the ultimate arbiter in conflicts among states, the threat of force obviously remains an instrument of international politics. The capacity to use military force is an element of national power and is related to a nation's power as the fist is to the body as the measure of strength for the individual. However, when force or violence is employed, it signifies the abdication of political power in favor of military power. The potentiality of armed strength is the most important material factor comprising a nation's political power; in overt conflict physical violence takes the place of psychological relations between two minds or political forces. Once war has ceased, nations resume their psychological relationship. Political power determines territorial changes which have resulted from warfare and are determined by residual military and political strength. Power expresses itself in peace settlements or agreements and its instrument is effective diplomacy, not the continued employment of force.

An opposing interpretation of the relationship between power and force has gained currency in the late 1970s and 1980s among some conservative leaders inspired by the Russian writer, Aleksander Solzhenitszn. Their views have not been subjected to much critical discussion. These writers make force a first, not a last, resort, because they doubt the efficacy of attempts to conduct foreign policy through the employment of political rather than military power. In this view, power is indeed a facade which may lightly cover, but can neither disguise nor substitute for the exercise of force and violence. This is so because the unremitting hostility of the adversary means that he can only be beaten; efforts to cajole, bargain with, or even peacefully coerce him (through such means as economic sanctions and the skillful use of other carrots and sticks) will inevitably fall victim to his hatred and contempt.

Disciples of this view of the world crisis find that " ... no reconciliation with communist doctrine is possible. The alternatives are either its complete triumph throughout the world or else its total collapse everywhere."[6] The exercise of political or economic power by the West has proven fruitless. "Communism will never be halted by negotiations. ... It can only be halted by force from without or disintegration from within."[7]

Solzhenitszn and his followers for all practical purposes proclaim a call to arms. They announce that the retreat of the West is coming to an end. "The whole thrust of American diplomacy has been directed to postponing any conflict . . . at the cost of progressively diminishing American strength."[8] The world is approaching a point where " . . . the brink may not have been reached, but it is already the merest step away."[9] Because the West failed to defend its outlying borders, "the nearer ones will have to be held." The conflict can be equated with the struggle with Hitler for: "Today the Western world faces a greater danger than that which threatened it in 1939."[10] For those who see the world from this perspective, we stand "on the eve of the global battle between world communism and world humanity"[11] and "there is an imminent danger of a takeover in Western Europe and many other parts of the world."[12] At so critical a point in world history, force is the sole defense against those who "believe that their hour of world conquest has arrived. . . . "[13] Power expressed in diplomatic or economic terms can no more prevent the victory of communism than Munich could halt Hitler or League of Nations sanctions turn back Mussolini. Indeed communism in the 1980s, compared with fascism's threatened domination of the whole world in the 1940s, is far down the road to achieving its goal.

The view that power is subordinated to force has not confined itself to the worldwide struggle with communism. It manifests itself also in the debate over American policy to free the hostages in Iran. According to this viewpoint, failure to use force is to blame for the decline of American influence over events affecting the captives. Every attempt to bring the weight of international authority to bear on the revolutionary government or to use economic or political pressures was doomed because of the demonic nature of the Islamic fundamentalist regime. The moral degradation of the enemy has spread throughout society to the point that retrograde leaders have placed themselves beyond the reach of any reasonable response to moral and political authority. Ironically, the spokesman for a policy of force vis-a-vis Iran in late 1979 and the first three quarters of 1980 had by the autumn of 1980 begun to call for sanctions against Iraq for aggression against Iran.

1. POWER

The brilliant diplomatic historian, Louis J. Halle, for more than twenty years a professor at the Graduate Institute of International Studies in Geneva, declares that the obstacle most crippling to understanding contemporary world politics is the absence of a theory of power and diplomacy. From agriculture to war, internationalists have in other spheres formulated general principles of international relations. Americans since World War II have made giant strides toward comprehending the international environment. No longer is national security defined in the language of isolationism or "Fortress America." Holding our hand until the eleventh hour was possible when the balance of power was anchored in Europe. Today as crises erupt around the world, it is the President or the Secretary of State who is awakened in the dead of night to speak for the West, not the leaders of Britain, France or West Germany. The doctrine of "no entangling alliances" foreshadowed in Washington's Farewell Address and made explicit in Jefferson's "First Innaugural," may have served the fledging nation; it can no longer provide guidelines for a country to become a world leader anymore than an American President can govern the nation from within without the support of political coalitions.

Professor Halle credits America's intellectuals and policymakers with having fashioned broadly acceptable ideas of international responsibility. He praises strategic theorists for having defined and elaborated the concept of deterrence, linking military force not with war-making but with offering incentives to an expansionist power to action through political or economic rather than military means. According to Halle, no operational theory has had so far-reaching an impact on postwar foreign policy as the idea of deterrence. The great powers who have pursued their objectives making use of limited force, the threat of force and proxy wars, but stopping short of general war, have done so primarily because of what Winston S. Churchill called the balance of terror. Among Americans, Bernard Brodie, Thomas Schelling and Albert Wolhstetter have defined deterrence more precisely and provided working principles. It is difficult to refute those who say that the world has known an uneasy global peace for thirty-five years in part because the superpowers have been deterred from war because of unacceptable damages which their opponent would impose if total war broke out.

If deterrence has made possible a precarious peace in the Cold War, it has not prevented political rivalries or international conflicts that involve military conflict or verge on war. If open warfare involving east and west has been prevented, limited wars have not. Between 1945 and 1969, there were approximately one hundred instances of limited, localized international warfare. However the gravamen of the Cold War, despite vast preparations for war, has been not warfare but a continuing unresolved power struggle. National and international leaders have been faced by a succession of clashes of interest and will which have been contained through power and diplomacy or through the use of force. Nations and sub-national groups in the first instance seek to impose their will through testing one another not by force of arms but by display of strength and power. The struggles between the Soviet Union and the United States, China and the Soviet Union, NATO and the Warsaw Pact and the industrial and less developed countries have involved continuous, ongoing struggles for power more often than open military conflicts and war. Peace has been maintained in Western Europe and between the United States and the Soviet Union despite the unremitting struggle for power.

While the persisting problem of the postwar era has been the struggle for power between east and west and more recently between north and south, the intellectual basis for dealing with the problem has been sorely lacking. One reason for this lack is the ambivalence of many Americans toward power, rejecting it for other alternatives but then in a crisis assuming that force was the only expression of power. Americans by nature shun power and especially theories of power, but in the words of a black militant find force and violence as "American as apple pie." In the immediate postwar period, American leaders framed their thinking on foreign policy by drawing a sharp line between war or peace. At the close of World War II, the United States cut national defense to the bone on the questionable assumption that total peace was destined to follow total war. In the last days of the war, American military and political leaders allowed Soviet armies to drive deep into the heart of Europe creating as grave an imbalance of power with Russia controlling Central Europe as if German forces had remained in the Soviet Union. American leaders by choosing to conceive the postwar world as having moved from total war to perpetual peace allowed Soviet power to be concentrated in Eastern and Central

Europe alongside power vacuums created by the devastation of the countries of Western Europe. Only gradually was a new balance of power established through what the historian Arthur Schlesinger, Jr. called "the brave and essential response of free men to communist aggression," through the Truman Doctrine, the Marshall Plan and NATO.

It is fair to ask the question, which is not without contemporary relevance, why Americans who organized a Grand Alliance in war failed in fashioning a structure of peace in the years immediately following that war. A first answer is that America saw peace and war as mutually exclusive alternatives. If we were not at war, we were at peace and peace required few of the sacrifices of war. Another answer is that one side fought the war for rather well-defined political and territorial objectives while the other postponed the quest for territorial and political settlements until the war was over, in effect, as far as Europe was concerned, until it was too late. Once the Red Army had marched into the center of Europe, only two means were possible theoretically, of reestablishing a balance of power. The one required the resumption of war against a wartime ally and the other negotiating the withdrawal of Soviet troops from their advanced position in Europe. Renewed warfare was impossible for both moral and military reasons; Soviet withdrawal became impossible once American forces had demobilized and the West negotiated from weakness. It had nothing to offer the Soviets in return for withdrawal. Winston S. Churchill grasped the problem posed by the two alternatives, but after his departure in the midst of the Potsdam talks only a handful of diplomatic analysts and a very few officials in government were predisposed to try to negotiate withdrawal.

While these several answers are all plausible, they are symptoms, not underlying causes of the American dilemma over power. Among the deeper, underlying causes, the most evident was the attitude toward power of some of the nation's most respected leaders, including influential intellectuals and a broad segment of public opinion. For them, thinking in terms of a balance of power and political and territorial objectives ran counter to certain deeply ingrained attitudes. Power politics was a dirty word; it was a condition to be eradicated by American leadership and by the dawn of a brave new world. Secretary of State Cordell Hull announced in 1943 on his return from the Moscow Conference that international organization would take the place of alliances, spheres of influence and the balance of power. A sense of urgency in building a structure of power as a condition of effective diplomacy was removed by those who heralded the birth of a new international order untarnished by the taint of power. When Churchill warned that an Iron Curtain had descended over all the ancient capitals of Europe on a line extending from Stettin to Trieste, he was denounced as the symbol of an old order. President Harry S. Truman, later to become the chief spokesman of resistance to Soviet expansion, chose to say he had not read the text of the Fulton Speech. From one side of the Atlantic, Mr. Harold Laski cried out: "Mr. Churchill is one of the great anachronisms of our time." On the other side, Norman Cousins proclaimed: "It is this counter direction, this retrogression, this reliance upon devices which have never...succeeded, that characterizes the general nature of [Mr. Churchill]'s approach]."

Events moved so swiftly, conditions involving east-west relations deteriorated so rapidly, that President Truman and his most influential advisers soon moved beyond Churchill in calling on Americans to oppose the spread of world communism. They were motivated less by recognition of the objective redistribution of power in Europe which followed World War II with the advance of the Soviet Union beyond the dreams of the Tsars, and more by successive crises beginning with Poland and including Greece, Turkey and Iran. It was Soviet actions that aroused Americans and led to a full turnabout in attitudes and policies. What compelled a change in perspective was not recognition that the brave new world was an illusion but rather a sense of betrayal by a trusted wartime ally.

America's most devoted friends warned we might be overreacting and for the wrong reason. On February 28, 1945, a young Conservative Member of Parliament, Captain Peter Thorneycroft, addressed the House of Commons saying:

> "I believe the real difficulty in which my hon. Friends find themselves is not so much Poland at all. I believe it is in the apparent conflict between documents like the Atlantic Charter and the facts of the European situation. We talk to two different people in two different languages. In the East we are talking to the Russians. The Russians are

nothing if not realists. . . . I believe that the Russian Foreign Office is perhaps more in tune with the advice which
would be given to the Tsars than to the potentates of the
twentieth century. In such circumstances we talk in
language not far removed from power politics. In the
West we are faced by the Americans. They are nothing if
not idealists. To them we talk in the polite language of the
Atlantic Charter. Somehow or other we have to marry
those two schools of thought. If I could persuade the
Americans, particularly in the Middle West, to have something of the Russian realism in international relations,
and persuade the Russians to have the idealism that exists
on the East coast of America, we might get somewhere,
but let us face the fact that the process will be a long and
painful one. You do not move suddenly from a world in
which there are international rivalries into a world where
there is international cooperation. It is the world that we
are in that the Prime Minister has to deal with. We could
not come back from Yalta with a blueprint for a new
Utopia. . . . The rights of small nations are safeguarded by
a mixture of diplomacy and military power. . . . "

2. POWER AND DIPLOMACY

A second enduring element of foreign policy, then, is diplomacy. If
this is a truism, it is one which has not obtained widespread
popular acceptance. Part of the problem in adjusting to the world
stems from recurrent doubts that power and diplomacy are lasting
features of international politics. One source of uncertainty about
the need for diplomacy is the triumph of constitutionalism on the
American scene. It is possible to argue that the American political
system is history's most notable social and political invention paral-
leling if not surpassing all the great technological inventions. (Natural
scientists have been known to taunt social scientists about the
paucity of their inventions but the American constitution surely
compares with any scientific or technical invention.) Reasoning
from this achievement, the conclusion follows that ideals and
institutions that have brought relative peace and stability to certain
people nationally can do the same for peoples internationally.

George F. Kennan has described this faith as " . . . the belief that it should be possible to suppress the chaotic and dangerous aspirations of governments in the international field by the acceptance of some system of legal rules and restraints." Overlooked is the necessity for community and moral consensus as prerequisites for law and government. It is the essence of this faith, that international law and organization can be substitutes here and now for diplomacy. The inevitability of conflicting national interests and the necessity of dealing with them piecemeal on their merits hoping to find the solutions least unsettling to international life has revived contemporary diplomacy. The assumption of those who would be done with diplomacy had been that "the things for which other peoples in this world are apt to contend are for the most part neither creditable nor important and might justly be expected to take second place behind the desirability of an orderly world, untroubled by international violence." (Kennan) This viewpoint is diametrically opposed to the assumption underlying traditional diplomacy that rivalry and some form of strife are the rule and the normal condition of world politics and not a mere historic accident of a backward and archaic past.

In all social groups within and outside constitutional systems, a contest for influence and power goes on but on the international scene rivalries are less controlled by effective law or government. Nations are not subject to a single sovereign authority. The task of foreign policy and diplomacy when national interests conflict is to limit struggles if possible through legal rules or moral maxims but inescapably through establishing effective balances of power or conditions of rough equilibrium among rival states. When interests conflict and legal rules go unrecognized or are in dispute, such disputes can only be mediated through diplomatic accommodation and adjustment and through restraint produced by the mutual recognition of an equilibrium of power. Compromises and bargaining reflecting a counterpoise of power and the application of checks and balances in a half anarchic world may prove the only practical means for mitigating inescapable international rivalries. The acceptance of compromise may appear less ennobling than the invoking of moral principles but a war postponed through the relaxation of tensions is oftentimes a war prevented in the future. What is essential for states is often necessary for individuals. Even within society's most intimate community, the family, harmony results from the mutual recognition of each member's most deeply held values and interests. And in relations among families, the poet Robert Frost wrote that "good fences make good neighbors."

The first difficulty in blending power and diplomacy stems, therefore, from an unwillingness to recognize their recurrent and perennial character. Neither religion nor education, law nor organization, peace nor prosperity have done away with the need for power and diplomacy among states. A second difficulty arises from the difficulty of making wise, objective and prudent estimates of power, essential to the success of diplomacy. Former Secretary of State Henry Kissinger singled out the estimating of America's power and that of its adversaries and friends in a given conflict as his most difficult, perplexing and exacting responsibility. One cause of this difficulty results from the conflicting perspectives of those who conduct foreign policy.

Harold Nicolson, the twentieth century's profoundest student of diplomacy, characterized diplomacy in the West as essentially of two types. One he called heroic diplomacy associated with the military viewpoint and with victory or defeat. The other is commercial or bourgeois diplomacy which he associated with classical or traditional diplomacy. Heroic diplomacy, he said, always seeks to maintain a preponderance of power, not an equilibrium, as a prerequisite of diplomacy. Commercial diplomacy recognizes that for every advantage there must be a disadvantage, for every gain some tradeoff. Merchants are more prepared than militarists to live in the everyday world of give and take. Nicolson maintained that all the great historic successes in diplomacy have had some element of commercial diplomacy about them and, for both parties, some give and take. If this were not so, diplomats and politicians whose stock and trade is compromise and bargaining would not be enlisted in the quest for peace. Otherwise we could think entirely of victory and defeat which has tended to be the stock and trade not only of military men but of social reformers as well.

A corollary of Nicolson's ideas about diplomacy relates to the actors who determine foreign policy, especially in a democracy. The problem with almost every public and foreign policy debate today, is that men who must necessarily be on tap tend inevitably, with all the technical and scientific complexities of estimating power, to move to the top. Technical issues for important sectors of decision making are beyond the ordinary citizen's comprehension. This is true when the President calls on economists to advise on inflation and when he calls in authorities on welfare, housing, minorities or health. It is true to an even greater extent when Americans engage in a great debate on foreign policy against a background of nuclear weapons of assured mutual destruction. Confusion for laymen in the military field is multiplied when the same military advisors who had earlier described the atomic bomb as equivalent to a hundred and seventy-five Russian divisions, now argue that nuclear weapons are today no different than any other weapons. This type of discrepancy and contradiction keeps entering the debate over SALT and START and over military preparedness and civil defense and is not easily resolved.

Thus, while military and technical people, including nuclear scientists, must always be called on to advise on the components of power with which they are familiar and must be on tap to serve the President, the American people can rest easier knowing that in a civilian government, they need not necessarily be on top. It is worth reminding ourselves in any great debate over the issues at stake in public policy that the requirements and predispositions of the professional position we occupy lead us to take stands and sponsor views which are shaped by our assigned function and the role we have come to play.[14]

In such instances, there may be good reason for calling to mind Cromwell's famous injunction: "I beseech you, in the bowels of Christ, to think it possible you may be mistaken." It is worth remembering that many of the people who warned of the bomber gap in the 1950s, the missile gap in 1960 and the possibilities of an ABM gap five or ten years later, are the same type of people who now ask, with impressive credentials and polemical force that we follow their views with regard to SALT II or START. They may be right about SALT or START, having been wrong before, but they might in the fervor do well to remember Cromwell's. words. Their former mistakes which subsquently came to light, included claims regarding a fictitious bomber gap which led to a buildup by the United States in nuclear armed heavy bombers— the B-47 and then the B-52—only to discover that the Soviet heavy bomber force was more modest in size than they had estimated. The missile gap which candidate John F. Kennedy, following his best military advice, had used in his campaign against President

Eisenhower and which led to the resulting large-scale production of Minuteman and Polaris strategic missiles, later proved to have been based on exaggerated if not false estimates. The price for being wrong was a rapid increase in arms buildups on both sides.

Fortunately, in every military and foreign policy debate, a diversity of views emerge and in the end the appropriate governmental authorities must reach a judgment. They must weigh the views of scientists like Edward Teller against those of President Eisenhower's Assistant for Science and Technology, George Kistiakowsky, of military men like Admiral Zumwalt against General Andrew Goodpaster. In the process, they must judge political and economic consequences as well as military advantages.

A third difficulty in the estimates a statesman must make of power is its many-sided character or the multiple dimensions of power. I reviewed the book, *The Third World War,* which has become a best seller. Alongside the immense scientific and technical knowledge contained in the book, I found unbelievable political naivety and unconcealed foreign policy ignorance. It seemed rather curious that the authors, a group of outstanding NATO military men, would offer a scenario in which our principal and most effective ally in the decisive final struggles in the Middle East turning the tide of battle in World War III was the Shah of Iran. The book completed a few months before the Shah's overthrow suggests not a trace of awareness of momentous changes in the political and social order in Iran. The moral may be that if military strength is the foremost quantitative index of power, then politics, national morale and the quality of government and diplomacy are the most important qualitative elements of power, to say nothing of factors as impalpable as national prestige. To equate Hitler with Stalin, and certainly with Brezhnev or Chernenko, is to be ignorant of politics and foreign policy and to forget that for almost forty years, we have looked East and seen a military power of enormous strength with divisions overwhelmingly outnumbering ours. (We tend to forget in such comparisons that Hitler's advances occurred a few brief years after he came to power.) By contrast to this hour, the mighty forces of the Soviet Union have not crossed into Western Europe and initiated military conflict. Those who explain all this in terms of earlier American nuclear superiority have an obligation to explain how nuclear parity or Soviet superiority, which according to differing estimates now exist, has not brought about an invasion of

Western Europe. To equate, as the critics of SALT II were wont to do, the intrusion by Cuban troops armed by the Russians into Angola with the invasion of the Rhineland by Hitler is from the standpoint of the world balance of power to make a mockery of any kind of discriminate military and political judgment. It suggests such critics are advocates first and analysts second.

We need also to recall that the failures leading up to World War II were not alone failures of military preparation and military action. They were also political failures, as Arnold Wolfers and Hans J. Morgenthau pointed out, of the allies and of France and Britain in particular, to concert their foreign policies and present any kind of united, consistent and coherent opposition which carried weight with Hitler, rather than tempting him with the disunity of the West. In sum, we make an enormous mistake now, not only in Europe but in the Third World, to whom we preach non-proliferation and the abandonment of non-alignment, if we imagine that by talking exclusively about military and technological factors we have exhausted the foreign policy agenda. There are other impalpable, intangible political factors that must be thrown on the scales in estimates of power.

A fourth and final difficulty in the estimates of power concerns those who have the right to be heard, who speak authoritatively to the public on power and policy. One particularly vocal critic of SALT II argued that American people who favor SALT agreements have been mislead by amateurs and charlatans. He made the point that if someone is ill he seeks a qualified physician, if in litigation he calls on a recognized attorney. By the same token in matters of national security, he ought to turn to an expert on national defense. This analogy demands scrutiny in at least two important respects. First, no one seeking advice on widely debated issues of national security is likely to find his own private physician. Because military men and prominent scientists feel deeply about national defense, they take to the hustings when out of power to rally support for their views. They tend to become not private advisors like physicians but public advocates, some in support of the administration they serve and others waging the good fight in public on policies they have defended but on which they have fought losing battles within successive administrations. A more apt analogy than that of the best qualified physician counselling the citizenry on defense is that of two physicians who have offered the patient opposing diagnoses. After the patient has chosen to follow one, assuming the patient is the administration, the physician who has been spurned decides to go public with his diagnosis.

Identifying the expert on national defense with the physician is defective in another respect. If foreign policy were simply a matter of military strategy, the debate would be quickly resolved. Foreign policy estimates, whatever else they involve, require the best informed judgments a government can muster of both *capabilities* and *intentions*. Not only must every chief executive and his principal advisors in the United States seek two kinds of broad-gauged estimates but so must the leaders of every other regime who would formulate policies based on reason not emotion. It should be obvious that not everyone qualified to assess capabilities is equipped by training and concerns to judge intentions and the obverse is equally true. A chief executive and a government must look not to one physician but to at least two kinds of physicians with different competences and skills. The one physician can speak to capabilities and realistic defense requirements while the other must analyze a nation's intentions, its historic national interests, change and continuity in its policies and trends, and directions within society as a whole and must do so in the most difficult setting of a culture which is not his own.

So powerful is the force of modern day nationalism, that every nation's policymakers are characteristically disposed to emphasize one or the other aspect of foreign policy, to talk either of capability or intentions as it serves their purpose and fills out their picture of the world, to invoke one or the other concept in foreign policy rhetoric. Thus Americans who arm the Turks, the Iranians, the Israelis, the Saudis or the Egyptians hasten to reassure anxious nations, whether sometime friends or foes, not to judge us or our friends by capabilities but by intentions. We say the Soviets have no reason to evaluate U.S. policy by our regional or worldwise capabilities or those of our allies but by the absence on *our* side of any aggressive military intentions. Yet we judge the Soviets, especially in recent months, by *their* growing capabilities. What if the Soviets were to send $8 billion in arms to Mexico as we have to Iran and Saudi Arabia? Would we assume the buildup of so vast a capability on our doorstep reflected a benign intention?

Historically, Americans have formulated foreign policies that rested on the best available estimates of both capabilities and intentions. We have had outstanding military men of proven character and integrity with the ability and resources to assess capabilities, but also foreign policy experts—for example, diplomats such as Charles Bohlen, Llewelyn Thompson, Malcolm Toon and George F. Kennan in Moscow—with the knowledge and background for assessing intentions. While neither group has been infallible, the nation has turned both to its most trusted military and its foreign policy analysts precisely because we have recognized that together, not apart, they possessed the physicians' knowledge in understanding the international body politic. It is not enough to depend on diplomatic or political analysts nor enough to depend on military analysts. In wartime, we make use of Order of Battle officers some of whom look at enemy fire power and others who try to assess the political loyalties and ideological fanaticism of enemy units. Similarly in peacetime, we turn to foreign policy authorities who, for example, analyze a period of change in the Soviet Union with origins in the period from 1954 to 1963 as does Professor Stephen F. Cohen of Princeton when he writes:

> Soviet Russia has been on our minds—a virtual obsession—for [more than] . . . sixty years. During these sixty years, far more has changed in the Soviet Union . . . than in our perceptions and ideas.[15]

The failure of our perception of Soviet intentions, according to Cohen, derives from widespread misconceptions and misreading of Soviet domestic factors. In his words: "Our focus on the continuing authoritarianism and the political abuse in the Soviet Union, obscures the fact that during the Khrushchev years there occurred in that country an authentic political and social reformation. Virtually every area of Soviet life was affected by these changes, however contradictory and ultimately limited. . . . " The conservative reaction which began during Khruschev's later years in power and intensified after his overthrow in 1964 continues today. In any other society, this reaction would appear normal—a period of reform followed by a conservative backlash. As a physician of Soviet domestic life, Cohen identifies three competing trends which are evident over the past 25 years, especially at the middle and upper levels of the Communist Party: the reformist, conservative and neo-Stalinist or reactionary trends. The reformers are today the weakest element numerically and in influence. Only if there were a progressive relaxation of tensions between the USSR and its foreign adversaries could they regain the influence they began to exercise under Khrushchev. Since the mid 1960's, conservatives have predominated and they range from sincere believers in the status quo to cynical defenders of vested bureaucratic interests. A third group, the reactionaries, yearn for the restoration of Russian chauvinism and Stalin's despotism short of mass terror remembering Beria's fate. All three groups are nationalistic, loyal to the party system and fearful of China. Like politics everywhere, Soviet politics has its share of political coalitions. Reformers and conservatives appear to favor some form of *detente* and expanding economic relations with the West but reactionaries and conservatives unite on cultural and intellectual policy and on means of preserving and extending Soviet influence and power. In important areas and especially in domestic affairs, Brezhnev moved, especially since the breakdown of SALT talks and America's *de facto* alliance or expanding friendship with China, toward the neo-Stalinists while seeking through *detente* and a kind of defensive imperialism, to preserve power and prestige at home and abroad. It would be idle to speculate on the eventual outcome of this three-way struggle but equally mistaken to ignore its effects on Soviet intentions.

One other factor influences Soviet intentions and must be considered and weighed however much it involves reasoning within "the infirm substance of imponderables." Cohen explains: "Soviet leadership for all its gains as a great power since 1945 can find little solace in foreign policy achievements. There is a perceived menace of China; the recalcitrant empire in Eastern Europe, which has been the scene of a major crisis every decade; the advent in Western Europe of so-called Euro-communist parties, whose success threatens to complete the de-Russification of international communism; the familiar problem of third world "allies," who become fickle or difficult to control, as in Egypt and India; and the staggering costs of a global competition however peaceful with the United States. The main thing to be said about these problems is not that they portend an imminent crisis but they represent long term and hopelessly intertwined dilemmas and impose severe constraints on domestic and foreign policy, and that there is [within Russia] no real majority view as to their solution."[16] Add to these dilemmas the problems of

Soviet authority in Afghanistan and Poland and the picture is complete.

Therefore, American leaders must be attentive to Soviet military capabilities while at the same time seeking to penetrate Soviet intentions. What we do in the realm of diplomacy and at efforts at arms control will have its influence on the three-way struggle of forces within the Soviet Union. Observing the rising influence of the military viewpoint in America since Iran and Afghanistan, we ought not be surprised by the rise and fall of certain groups in the Soviet Union. If we confine the debate to estimates of military hardware or heed only the physician who speaks of capabilities, we shall blind ourselves to what may be happening or could happen or might be assisted to happen within the Soviet Union affecting intentions. If we listen only to the military strategist and ignore the voice of the diplomatist, we shall proceed with life and death decisions on the faulty basis of half-knowledge. We shall use only half the intelligence available to us in these difficult times. The Soviet military buildup and the movement of its forces are realities. The Soviets have never foresworn wars of national liberation; the present era at best will be one of "partial detente," not detente oversold and packaged as bringing an end to Cold War rivalries. If the signals by which we measure Soviet intentions are unclear, the Soviets may be uncertain of our intentions voiced by three administrations and what they interpret as anti-trade, anti-SALT, and anti-regime reinforced by pro-military and pro-China pressures throwing shadows over consistency in American foreign policy.

It is difficult to believe, given all the problems which confront both the Soviet Union and the United States, that any rational evaluation of each other's intentions could lead either to conclude that its adversary was successfully embarking on the conquest of the whole world. Americans know all too well the constraints of inflation and the dollar, a volunteer army and the post-Vietnam syndrome and a weakened national consensus—and the Soviets are not oblivious to American problems. Informed Americans who look inside Russia report labor and housing shortages, the demoralization of youth, drunkeness, agricultural inefficiency, poor health care, aging leadership, disproportionate population growth among non-Slavic minorities, Moslem unrest, resurgent nationalism and labor unrest in Eastern Europe and uncertainties over each succession. However Americans may differ in their estimates of ultimate

Soviet intentions, they may be able to agree that despite mounting armament programs, the Soviets are destined in any foreseeable future to pursue their goals from overall weakness, not from overwhelming strength. Power, declared Reinhold Niebuhr, is not military power alone but involves the strength of the body politic. Military capacity for the nation corresponds to the fist for man. Power depends on the health and vitality of the whole body which gives the fist its striking power. If any part of the body is weakened or diseased, the fist becomes impotent. Nor are the Soviets alone subject to this constraint. Power and diplomacy are inextricably joined because successful diplomacy registers situations of power. Yet as Secretary Kissinger has argued, the diplomat has no more exacting task than in evaluating situations of power and he might have added the task begins with his answering the question "what is power?"

3. DIPLOMACY AS A CHANNEL OF POWER

In answering the question, a beginning can be made by suggesting what power is not, particularly for the 1980's. It is not a fixed quantity of some material substance that can be measured and displayed to the world once and for all. It is not alone military forces in being. If it were the United States would have been overwhelmed in World War II and by the Red Army in the postwar era. When we talk apocalyptically of 164 or more Soviet divisions, we need to remind ourselves that the Soviet Union in the early postwar period had 200 divisions on the borders of Europe. It is not industrial production gauged by pre-World War II standards such as coal and steel production or roads and harbors or refrigerators and household conveniences. Indeed too much affluence would seem to reduce power when a test of will was required. It is not numbers of people or geographic location nor is it standards of living or social welfare systems. It is not sending a gunboat up the rivers of an unfriendly state nor threatening to land the marines. It is not large missiles with multiple warheads nor smaller ones with greater precision. If it were, our military authorities would not vacillate as to which gives more power. It is not nuclear blackmail in a multipower world in which nuclear weapons have proliferated. It is not calling out to the world that America is number one nor imagining that in a moral sense we are living in the American century. It is not supposing that our ideas and institutions can quickly transform the world and do overnight what they have done for us.

If power is something more than any one of the prevailing concepts we apply in public debate, then what is it? One answer is that power is not an abstraction but a relationship. Men and nations bring power to bear through channels. It is a product of circumstances. It is variously shaped and formed in different fields of endeavor. Power is filtered through political parties and elections in politics; through productivity and profits in business; through constitutions, statutes and procedures in law; and through creeds and doctrines in religion. In the maintenance of peace and the ending of war, power is filtered through diplomacy. Down to the present, diplomacy remains the most consistently used channel through which statesmen work their will on one another and protect their interests. As every other channel through which power is exercised has its unique characteristics, diplomacy has its own peculiar form and qualities. In Satow's classic language, diplomacy is the application of tact and intelligence to the conduct of foreign relations. Diplomacy is a practical art. It requires public servants who can show restraint (Talleyrand warned "et surtout, pas trop de zele") or in General George Catlett Marshall's phrase men who who can "hold down their emotions" without indulging themselves the passions of an aroused public. Writing at the height of the Cold War, Dean Rusk warned: "We [shall] . . . fail miserably if we let our glands determine our action, decide that any agreement equals appeasement . . . say that any fight must end only in . . . unconditional surrender." Diplomacy envisages individuals of wisdom and courage coping with circumstances. To quote Winston S. Churchill: "The problem can seldom be calculated on paper alone and never copied from examples of the past. Its highest solution must be evolved from the eye and brain and soul of a single man, which . . . hour to hour we are making all the unweightable adjustments, no doubt with many errors, but with an ultimate practical accuracy." Walter Lippmann observed: "The reason why we trust one man rather than many, is because one man can negotiate and many can't."[17] "The worst kind of diplomatists," wrote Harold Nicolson, "are missionaries, fanatics and lawyers; the best kind are the reasonable and humane skeptics."[18] To this, Lippmann added: "One diplomat may see what is in the other diplomat's mind, and time his utterance accordingly; a whole people cannot see quickly into another people's mind. . . . The very qualities which are needed for negotiation—quickness of mind, direct contact, adaptiveness, invention, the right proportion of give and take—are the very qualities which masses of people do not possess."[19]

Diplomacy provides a poultice for drawing the poison out of a conflict. Infection seldom yields to impatience. Diplomacy most of the time proceeds without any worldwide moral consensus and few generally accepted principles of law. In an era of intense nationalism and what one observer calls "false religion," there is utility in tedium. There is a time to act and a time to wait, a time to debate and a time to negotiate, a time to be firm and a time for conciliation. Wise diplomacy must distinguish between them. Diplomacy requires keeping the channels open between rival powers. It demands listening for signals. Leaders may in speeches, press conferences or interviews signal they are prepared to negotiate. The Berlin Blockade of 1948-49 was settled when Ambassador Philip C. Jessup successfully explored with the Russian Ambassador to the United Nations the meaning of a conciliatory statement by Stalin. Following the Cuban missile crisis, the hotline between Moscow and Washington enabled Kennedy and Khrushchev to communicate. Diplomacy in the conference rooms and anterooms of the United Nations has sometimes filled in the gaps between adversaries who had stopped talking. As anger and public feelings mount in a crisis, Americans need to remember that the Austrian Peace Treaty, the Korean Armistice and the Nuclear Test Ban Treaty each required hundreds of old-fashioned diplomatic meetings before agreements were hammered out. President Lyndon B. Johnson, having contemplated bombing North Korea to retaliate for the hijacking of the U.S. Pueblo, turned instead to diplomats and after eleven long months of negotiations, they won the release of 82 crewmen. It required three months of hard bargaining in London skillfully guided by the British Foreign Secretary Lord Carrington to persuade leaders of the Patriotic Front to accept a cease fire to end the Civil War in Zimbabwe-Rhodesia.

Diplomacy can be a means of buying time. In Churchill's words: "Circumstances change, combinations change, new groupings arise, old interests are superseded by new. Many quarrels that might have led to war have been adjusted." However time is not always on the side of peace and the same Churchill on December 10, 1948, rose in the Parliament to say: "I have frequently advised that we should endeavour to reach a settlement with Russia on fundamentally outstanding questions. . . . I believe that in this resides the best hope of avoiding a third world war." By the 1950's, Churchill had called on no less than forty occasions for an approach to the Russians aimed at a peaceful settlement. Future historians will judge whether Churchill or those who opposed him were right. Dwight D. Eisenhower with strong political support from Senators Walter George and Richard Russell was later to undertake "summit diplomacy" as Churchill proposed. The European settlement of which Churchill dreamed came much later in Willy Brandt's Ostpolitik and the Helsinki Accords.

What Churchill offered the world, however, was not only a viewpoint concerning the timing of diplomatic initiatives but a framework for considering the relationship between power and diplomacy. Surely Churchill needs no defenders as a champion of freedom. He stands supreme as the father of the doctrine that security comes only with strength and that the appetites of an aggressor feed on success. Yet it is often forgotten that he called in his Fulton Speech not only for resistance to Soviet expansion but for a settlement when he declared: "What is needed is a settlement, and the longer it is delayed, the more difficult it will be and the greater our dangers will become." Again on April 18, 1947, at Albert Hall he proclaimed: "I say with all sincerity that our policy towards Russia may be one of honourable friendship from strength." It would be difficult to think of a western statesman who so consistently tried to link power with diplomacy.

Finally, wise diplomacy is the channel through which orderly relations among nations are conducted and conditions of peace are enhanced. It is the route along which sovereign states historically have pursued their interests with one another. Diplomacy imposes a sense of limits. Statecraft provides an historical deposit of accumulated practical wisdom. It injects caution into the counsels of the mightiest world power. It offers reminders that to speak of "losing China" or "Iran" or "Afghanistan" is a form of moral preteniousness. Having said we would not dirty our hands with power politics, we and the Soviet Union—both of us relative newcomers in the ongoing game of great power politics and each caught in the grip of internal forces the other only partly understands—have played the power game with a vengeance seeking to control directly what others historically have sought to affect indirectly. A nation which uses its power to install a new regime must live with the consequences. When a foreign people take to the streets, they will condemn an unpopular ruler but even more an alien power who has too openly been his sponsor. Then the outside power has but two alternatives: war and repression or strategic withdrawal. The first is the alternative of a ruthless totalitarian regime (when Jan Masaryk was asked why his country made an alliance with the Soviet Union after the Second World War, he answered: I'd rather be taken prisoner by the Americans). The second is the course that democratic and freedom-loving states have characteristically followed awaiting the day when they could exercise influence again less obtrusively.

Diplomacy must rest on power but available power employed with discretion and sophistication. At one point, six battalions of the King's Rifles preserved order and stability against the mutiny of troops in East Africa with a thousand men in each battalion spread across vast expanses. Developments and changes in countries outside our jurisdiction yield slowly and imperceptibly to outside prompting and aid. The governments and societies of other lands are plants and not machines. We are not their maker. Like a gardener we can help improve the soil, guard against unfriendly neighbors, and pray for the grace of kindlier elements that time and events may bring to the fore.

4. POWER, FORCE AND DIPLOMACY

Nothing in the diplomatic equation removes the necessity of force which, given the likelihood that conflicts may get out of control, remains the final arbiter. It is true in a dangerously divided world that outbreaks of violence are not the exception, as with civil wars within integrated national societies, but the rule. Violence, as Arendt argued, is a last resort to keep power intact. Stalin's much quoted phrase, "how many divisions does the Pope have," suggests a stubborn fact of international politics. It would be as great a fallacy to exclude force from the foreign policy equation as to set aside power or diplomacy.

Yet force no more than power is not an end in itself but a means to safeguard underlying foreign policy objectives. Nations and their responsible leaders have an obligation to define their vital interests and decide what they are prepared to defend by force of arms and what they must strive to safeguard with other means. It could be argued that American obsession with the direct threat of Soviet Union led to policies in a Third World country like Iran that led to neglect of other considerations that might have prevented the emergence of violently anti-American attitudes in Iran. The lesson of Iran is not so much the issue of whether America supported or did not support the Shah enough before he was overthrown but whether policymakers failed to recognize the two requirements of American policy for Iran: the maintenance of a strategic balance in the region and the aspirations of the Iranian people.

Five principles regarding force in the 1980's are as vital for the policymaker in shaping foreign policy as are the items that make up a pilot's checklist as he prepares for flight at the end of the runway. First and more important than all the others in a nuclear age, the policymaker cannot forget that force has lost the simple rationale it possessed in all previous eras. War throughout history has constituted the pursuit of policy by other means. Today war, as Albert Einstein warned, carries the possibility of "mutual annihilation." Every President and Secretary of State has known this since the Soviets exploded their first atomic bomb; each has measured success by the avoidance of a nuclear holocaust. Periodically, the public in moments of war hysteria has been misled into thinking nuclear war would be no different than any other wars. Those who have retained some semblance of objectivity about the destructiveness of nuclear weapons have not indulged themselves such an illusion.

Second, the first principle being true, the credibility of the use of such force except in an action of last resort has diminished the effectiveness of the threat of force by the super powers. For this reason, smaller powers have been successful in resisting domination by the great powers. The United States in Vietnam and in all likelihood the Soviet Union in Afghanistan have been frustrated in bringing the full arsenal of devastating force to bear against a far weaker power. Especially in localized wars, which have been the only wars tolerated in the Cold War, the effects of nuclear weapons on the conflict between the warring nations have been negligible.

Third, force whether actual or potential as an instrument of foreign policy assumes importance as a means of avoiding miscalculation by the other side. To announce in advance that a nation will not use force is to tempt an aggressor whether in Korea when Secretary Acheson and General MacArthur described Korea as falling outside America's defense perimeter or at the outset of the hostage crisis in Iran when President Carter appeared to promise the Ayatollah Khomeyni the United States would not use force.

Fourth and balancing the third principle, a nation that threatens to use force when it lacks the means or ability to back up its threats endangers the peace more than if it had remained silent. In this respect the Truman Doctrine and NATO respecting Western Europe were credible whereas John Foster Dulles' liberation foreign policy for Eastern Europe proved a threat the United States was unable or unwilling to back up. (Liberation was more an electoral slogan than a well-considered policy as statements by Eisenhower and Dulles during the Hungarian Revolution were to attest.) The Carter Doctrine, in the absence of a greater military capacity in the Persian Gulf, may have more in common with liberation than containment as an American foreign policy. It resembled more the Eisenhower Doctrine of 1957 which led to American intervention in Lebanon in 1958.

Fifth, the invoking of force assumes the clear and unequivocal identification of the enemy and the threat the enemy presents to international peace and security. Solzhenitszn and some military leaders equate the Soviet Union with Nazi Germany. There are risks in invoking the lessons of history if the differences outweigh the similarities, if Soviet aggression in Afghanistan poses issues that differ substantially from Hitler's seizure of Czechoslovakia in 1938. While it is possible to point to the threat which both the Soviets and Hitler have posed to international stability and to the balance of power, the threat is not necessarily the same. The Soviets present the threat of a calculating aggressor; Hitler rode roughshod over his military and political advisors. The Soviet ideology assumes the inevitability of Marxism's triumph in the world but national interest more than ideology appears to provide a fairly constant guideline for Soviet foreign policy. Hitler thought so little about national interest that he allowed himself to be caught in a two-front war. Hitler might have been stopped until the late 1930's without too high a price and thereafter without threatening the destruction of the world. No one has proposed in the 1980's that it would be relatively easy for American forces to drive Soviet troops out of Afghanistan now or that the Soviet Union could be defeated in a nuclear war as Hitler was conquered in World War II without seriously threatening the survival of civilization. These differences underscore the limitations of force in the 1980's and the need for East and West to continue to seek various forms of accommodation of their power.[20]

NOTES

1. Hannah Arendt, *On Violence* (New York: Harcourt, Brace & World, 1969), p. 42.
2. Ibid., p. 47.
3. Ibid., p. 49.
4. Ibid., p. 56.
5. Hans J. Morgenthau, *Politics Among Nations,* 5th ed. (New York: Alfred A. Knopf, 1973), p. 32.
6. Aleksandr Solzhenitszn, "Misconceptions about Russia," *Foreign Affairs* 58 (Spring 1980): 820.
7. Ibid., p. 834.
8. Ibid., p. 821.
9. Ibid., p. 834.
10. Ibid.
11. Ibid.
12. Ibid., p. 820.
13. Ibid.
14. For twenty years, I worked for an international technical assistance agency, and in that role I was not very receptive to outside questioning and criticisms of technical assistance activities. I had little patience with the skepticism others expressed about the Green Revolution which my agency helped to initiate and sustain. We all become "true believers" when our professional competence is put to the test. See my *Foreign Assistance—A View from the Private Sector,* University of Notre Dame Press, 1972.
15. Stephen F. Cohen "Soviet Domestic Politics and Foreign Policy," *Common Sense in U.S.-Soviet Relations;* Washington, D.C.: American Committee on East-West Accord, 1978, p. 11.
16. Ibid., p. 13.
17. Walter Lippmann, *The Stakes of Diplomacy,* New York: MacMillan Company, 1915, p. 26.

18. Harold Nicolson, *Diplomacy,* London: Oxford University Press, 1939, p. 50.
19. Walter Lippmann, *op. cit.,* p. 27.
20. This chapter is based on an article which appeared in *The Review of Politics,* Vol. 43, No. 3, July 1981, pp. 410–435.

The Churches and the Challenge of Peace: The Pastoral Letter on War and Peace

The twentieth century has been an era of devastating conflict with two worldwide conflagrations. Their outbreak led the historian Arnold J. Toynbee to describe the century as one in which Western Civilization suffered a double knockout blow. From the standpoint of continuous conflict, Toynbee found historical parallels with the two wars of the Romans and the Carthaginians and the two struggles of the Peleponnesian Wars. Spiritually and materially, twentieth century war has become "total war" in which the energies and emotions of whole populations are mobilized. Qualitatively, war has been transformed as participants seek the destruction of the enemy—as with unconditional surrender. Quantitatively, the scale and magnitude of warfare and the proportion of the population involved has expanded. Gibbon's description of warfare in the eighteenth century as a "temperate and indecisive contest" seems as far removed from present day conflict as the dominant view of enlightenment thinkers that war like slavery was on the wane and would soon disappear.

The exuberant optimism of the eighteenth century stemmed from certain objective factors. War tended to be a sport of kings fought for limited objectives and within a broad framework of accepted rules of the game. Its course was determined by the strategic moves of rival princes inspired by the goal of achieving final victory with a minimum of loss. Rulers followed complicated and cunning principles aimed at overcoming an enemy without destroying him. Military actions was held in check by the attitude of rulers toward one another; they had more in common with one another than with the people they ruled. For these reasons, the historian Ferrerro wrote of the eighteenth century as "one of those peaks of human evolution which man painfully attains only to slide back once more."

Successor historians maintain that war as a temperate and well-mannered pastime disappeared under the impact of two great nineteenth century social forces: democracy and the industrial revolution. The French Revolution ushered in the *levee en masse;* Mirabeau warned the French National Assembly that representative governments could be more bellicose than monarchial regimes. Industrialization provided new and more terrible weapons of war. Democracy contributed "the lethal drive" which empowered their use. Yet the humane spirit of the eighteenth century died hard. The balance of power in the nineteenth century held back the spread of conflict. From the Battle of Waterloo to the Battle of the Marne, casualties in civil wars exceeded those in international wars. From 1815 to 1898, the period of warfare involving five or more great powers did not exceed eighteen months. The burden of war was contained as the relative size of armies declined as did casualties in relation to population.

However, certain trends which began in the nineteenth reached fulfillment in the twentieth century. Moral fervor and national hatred exploded in wars of national self-righteousness. Distinctions regarding the status of civilians and combatants painfully worked out over four centuries fell victim to obliteration bombing. Universal military conscription of entire populations became commonplace. With the dawn of the nuclear age, the prospect of total destruction burst on the consciousness of mankind everywhere. The evil of general war which for centuries had been considered as acceptable representing a continuation of diplomacy by other means now became intolerable. For the first time in modern history, rational men asked the question which men had been asking in recent decades regarding crime in the streets that it is not unthinkable to respond to the threatening challenge "your money or your life" by answering "I surrender my money and save my life." Yet however rational the question and logical the answer, doubts persist whether a nation or its responsible leaders can respond in this way. So sudden has been the change in the nature of war that while ancient approaches may not be sufficient, credible new designs have not emerged as widely understood or accepted answers.

1. FORESHADOWINGS OF THE PASTORAL LETTER

The most recent appeal for national self-restraint and a far-reaching transformation of thinking for an unprecedently dangerous era is the bishops' letter. It is not the first time leaders have been called on to transcend traditional views of national strategy. Twentieth century foreshadowings of the letter include both statements by world councils and papal encyclicals grounded in religious faith and political and social proposals that have taken on a quasi-religious character. From Kant to Woodrow Wilson, democratic idealists have maintained that because democracies cherish peace, the eradication of war depends on multiplying the numbers of representative governments. A handful of troublemakers and aristocratic regimes have disrupted the natural harmony of free peoples. Once every nationality and ethnic group realizes self-determination, peace will be assured. Ironically, Hitler invoked this principle enshrined in the Versailles Treaty to justify reuniting the Sudetan Germans with the Fatherland. Nor did the creed of national self-determination prevent World War II.

The Wilsonian corollary of national self-determination was faith in world organization. The rock on which Wilson built his faith was the belief that "national purposes have fallen more and more into the background and the common purposes of enlightened mankind have taken their place." Yet the American Senate rejected Wilson's "Grand Design" and Britain and France proved unable to concert their policies within or outside the League. The Axis powers swept through Europe and the League was powerless to protect the weak. In the interwar period, the religious community joined other right-minded Americans to assure that never again would the United States turn aside from supporting international organization. However not only has the United Nations, in the absence of great power unanimity, been unable to maintain international security but twice in the decade Americans rather than men of lesser faith have withdrawn from United Nations agencies. As recently as the fall of 1983, our deputy ambassador to the United Nations invited the members if they were dissatisfied to remove the organization from American soil. In a few brief decades, the journey of the faithful has followed its tortuous path from the fervent faith of Wilson to the peevish retort of Ambassador Lichtenstein. If one can draw any lesson from the scorn heaped on international organization by latter day statesmen it is the inevitability of history following its accustomed course from illusions to disillusionment. No more than national self-determination has international organization proved a transforming force. We know now, if we did not at San Francisco, that the United Nations mirrors the forces and trends at work outside its walls. In this it merely recapitulates the life story of the League of Nations and every past international organization.

Finally, what has distinguished the postwar era is faith in two other forms of universalism, science and economic interdependence. To the question can science save us, many westerners have answered with a qualified yes. Scientists speak one another's language across national boundaries. Science binds the nationals of different countries together in the strongest present day universalism. It was the scientists of the Manhattan Project who first perceived the threat of worldwide destruction. More controlling than their national origin, common devotion to truth led them to launch the Bulletin of Atomic Scientists with its warning clock marking off the minutes before midnight.

However UNESCO which had its origins in Huxley's faith in the universality of science has floundered and become perhaps the most politicized of all international organizations. When Bertrand Russell called for scientists to replace statesmen to guarantee the peace of the world, he forgot that only the latter are bound by an official oath of office to preserve the union. He ignored the differences between the freedom of scientists and the responsibility of statesmen. Also he did not foresee that scientists would align themselves on both sides of the great debates over nuclear questions as with Kistiakowsky and Teller.

What national self-determination and international organization promised in earlier decades, economic interdependence holds out to the faithful in the later years of the postwar world. Those who look ahead point out that today's world is linked by networks of common economic interests, that problems can no longer be solved by struggling nation states. The work of a series of postwar economic conferences—Bretton Woods, GATT and the European Community—confirmed this fact and the International Monetary Fund and the World Bank appeared to institutionalize it. President Jimmy Carter, reflecting the views of his advisors, declared in a speech at Notre Dame that economic problems were coming to take the place of political ones. But with the Soviet invasion of Afghanistan, his administration came full circle. By the time he left office, President Carter had significantly increased military expenditures, embargoed grain shipments to the Soviet Union, withdrawn from the Moscow Olympics, proclaimed the Carter Doctrine for the Middle East and organized the rapid deployment force, all actions that hardly confirmed the primacy of global economic over national security interests. However bright the light of economic interdependence has shone, power continues to reside with national decision makers as it did with Saudi Arabia in the oil crisis of 1973. If the world is one economically, its fate is determined by representatives who speak for their nation states, not the world.

The gravaman of the lesson to be drawn from the threefold experiences of the foreshadowings of the Pastoral Letter is at best sobering for the prospects of national restraint.

2. FALLING BACK TO REALITY

The gulf that has continued to separate universal visions and hard realities has driven statesmen back to ancient truths about international relations. Political realism which was essentially discarded by those who glimpsed the foreshadowings of a new world has been revived. Among its tenets are the proposition that nations in a half-anarchic international society must give priority to their own interests and interests are defined in terms of power. National interest persists as a determinant of what national leaders accept and do. Realism calls for distinctions between the morally desirable and the politically possible. It asks for understanding that while prophets or reformers are free to construct an ideal world, statesman must be bound by distinctions between the desirable and the possible. While reformers can demand moral reasoning based on a brave new world, political leaders must make choices in the existing world. National security and preserving the union set boundaries of action for national decision makers.

The pastoral letter not surprisingly has a powerful strain of realism running through it. The reformist critic has not been slow to throw a searchlight on this dimension of the letter. He finds even qualified approval of deterrence as a means of preserving the peace wholly unacceptable. How can any religious leader give his blessing to the maintenance of a deterrent force made up of weapons capable of universal destruction? Or indeed of conventional forces composed of instruments of unparalleled destructiveness?

To those who offer such criticism, traditionalists defend the pastoral letter in the language of realism. For almost four decades, peace has been maintained in the world through the maintenance of a stable deterrent force in the West. No one can say whether it might also have been preserved in the absence of deterrence. What is known is that general war involving the Soviet Union and the United States has not occurred despite flashpoint crises in Berlin, Korea, Cuba, Czechoslovakia, Hungary and the Middle East. Recognizing the fact of war not having broken out between the superpowers during a period in which each recognized the other's effective deterrent, it is asking a lot of their leaders to gamble on the possible consequences of abandoning deterrence. The bishops must have recognized this. Evidently they struggled as much over the language they used about deterrence as over any other issue. Finally, they found deterrence "morally acceptable" not as an end in itself but as a step on the way toward progress in reducing nuclear arsenals. In other words, deterrence was linked with negotiations for arms control.

What is most striking about this formulation, apart from the fact that it satisfies neither pacifist nor militarist critics, is that it places the bishops squarely alongside realist statesmen and thinkers. Those who describe Winston S. Churchill as an uncompromising foe of communism sometimes forget that, beginning with his Fulton Speech, he called on no fewer than some fifty occasions for negotiations between east and west. Alongside his warning that the West must prepare itself to resist Russian expansionism, he also warned that matters must not be allowed to drift but leaders must meet at the Summit. Speaking of the atomic bomb and American strength, he reminded fellow Conservatives: "We must not be in any doubt as to what is preserving the peace and security of the world. . . . " Yet there was more to deterrence than the West's strength. He declared in the House of Commons:

> There never was a time when the deterrents against war were so strong. The penalties have grown to an extent undreamed of; and at the same time, many of the old

incentives which were the cause of the beginning of so many wars . . . have lost their significance. The desire for glory, booty, territory, dynastic or national aggrandizement; hopes of a speedy and splendid victory with all its excitement . . . are now superseded by a preliminary stage of measureless agony from which neither side could at present protect itself.

But then Churchill added: "Moralists may find it a melancholy thought that peace can find no nobler foundation than mutual terror. But for my part, I shall be content if these foundations are solid, because they will give us the extra time and the new breathing space for the supreme effort which has to be made for a world settlement."

For Churchill as for the bishops, deterrence and negotiations were linked. It would be claiming too much to say that the relative emphasis the British leader and the bishops give to the two sides of the equation are the same or that they would phase in and out of deterrence and diplomacy in the same way. What ranges them together within a common tradition is recognition that deterrence and improving the objective conditions making deterrence necessary are interconnected. At Fulton, Missouri, Churchill said: "What is needed is a settlement and the longer it is delayed, the greater our dangers will become." Is there not every likelihood that if he were alive today he like the bishops would be in search of means of reducing tensions?

3. REALISM WITH A DIFFERENCE

The bishops would appear to have followed not only the strictures of secular realists but of Pope John Paul who observed that: "in this world a totally and permanently peaceful human society is unfortunately a utopia, and that ideologies that hold up that prospect as easily attainable are based on hopes that cannot be realized, whatever the reason behind them." Because utopias lie beyond reach, men of affairs must search out practical moral guideposts in an imperfect world. Moreover, the imperfect world of the 1980s is not that of the 1930s or 1940s. It is a world Albert Einstein envisaged when he said in 1945 that the atomic bomb had changed everything except "our modes of thinking." Realism for the 1980s must be realism with a difference because the destructive power of nuclear weapons requires a fundamental rethinking of the relation of military force to politics and morals. On this issue, profound differences have arisen between realists such as George F. Kennan, the late Hans J. Morgenthau and Reinhold Niebuhr and others including those whom a sharp tongued critic recently referred to as "the hired guns" of the administration.

Realism with a difference starts with the proposition that "keeping the peace in the nuclear age is a moral and political imperative." The bishops voice this imperative with a sense of urgency greater than that which stems from the historic presumption of Catholic teaching against war. Traditionally, just war doctrines had justified the use of force in self defense in exceptional cases. The church has recourse to a revered just war tradition which provides standards through which states are justified in waging war: The cause must be just, the authority legitimate and resort to force a last resort. Conceivably, a nation embarking on a nuclear war might meet some or all of these tests. Those who justify limited nuclear war rest their case in part on these criteria.

More fundamental, however, than the three standards is the principle of proportionality, a concept that just war theorists and traditional political realists alike accept. The damage to be inflicted and the costs of war must "be proportionate to the good expected by taking up arms." By this standard alone, nuclear war is ruled out as is the prophecy by defense officials that one superpower or the other can prevail. It is nearly impossible to foresee a situation in which nuclear conflict would not result in such widespread devastation in human lives and material resources as to place its justification on the principle of proportionality beyond rational calculation.

A more controversial application of just war doctrine but one that is examined in the bishops' letter is the principle of discrimination. War must be directed "against unjust aggressors not against innocent people caught up in a war not of their making." The bishops declare: "Under no circumstances may nuclear weapons or other instruments of mass slaughter be used for the purpose of destroying population centers or other predominantly civilian targets."

Critics address two questions to the authors of the letter which focus on the principle of discrimination. First, is it not the lesson of

World War II that all contemporary warfare in which major powers are involved tends to become indiscriminate? It would be difficult to prove for either side that "innocent lives" were not taken of "people who were in no way responsible for reckless actions of their governments." Second, some writers on force and defense analysts have argued that the West must not "forego the option of using them (nuclear weapons) discriminately." They argue:

> Since nuclear weapons, their technological develop-
> ment, and production cannot be abolished by disarma-
> ment agreements (and we might not welcome the resulting
> reduction of mutual deterrence and the increased insta-
> bility of the military balance, if they were), moral respon-
> sibility and practical prudence dictate that we develop
> strategies, weapons, and operational controls that maxi-
> mize the possibility of using nuclear exchanges as rational
> instruments of policy rather than as self-defeating un-
> controllable instruments of catastrophe. This requires dis-
> criminating counterforce capabilities, effective command,
> control and communications systems, and early war-
> termination strategies to accompany war-fighting capa-
> bilities.[1]

The main burden of the views of the critic quoted above is that technical competence, sophisticated reasoning and calculated prudence can serve nations in the formulation of strategy in the nuclear age as they have throughout history. What separates the two viewpoints is precisely their differences here. For the bishops, new "modes of thought" are required while for the critics "old modes" suffice. There is irony in the fact that representatives of one of the world's oldest traditions should call for new ways of thinking.

The "new modes of thought" involve, first, an explicit recognition that present necessities of state are conditional and temporary. An example is the conditioned moral acceptance of deterrence by the bishops who add that they "cannot consider such a policy adequate as a long-term basis for peace." Deterrence must be balanced by negotiations and disarmament. It is not an end in itself but a means toward the end of arms control. What the bishops resist more than anything else is the perception of military values as absolutes however legitimate they may be. To avoid making military values absolute, they must be viewed as relative and conditional, "relative to the fundamental need of civilization for survival, conditional on the observance of those elementary moral scruples beyond which horror becomes unlimited and hope impossible."[2]

Second, the bishops make plain that they oppose the production of new weapons simply because nations possess the knowhow. The late Rene Dubois criticized technological determinism by which he meant society's building ever larger missiles or warships because the technology was at hand. Former Secretary of State Dean Rusk observed that "we are beginning to hear talk about reviving antiballistic missiles. . . . But the development of ABMs in the form of missiles carrying nuclear or conventional warheads makes no sense whatever. Any schoolboy knows that the presence of such ABMs on both sides would simply cause each side to multiply its offensive weapons to the point where ABMs could be smothered or used up before the main strikes were developed."[3] Rusk applies the same form of reasoning to weapons development in outer space. Having noted a certain jubilation among Pentagon officials at the time of the first successful shuttle flight, Rusk warned against launching an arms race in space "that would stagger the imagination in terms of cost, add little or nothing to comparative military capabilities and merely provide a massive subsidy to the aerospace industry."[4]

Third, the bishops are highly skeptical about the possibility and the real meaning of limited nuclear war. At first glance, it seems plausible to argue that "the brightest prospect for moral improvement in the management of force lies not in avoiding or abolishing force but in carefully cultivating the modalities for limiting and controlling force—including nuclear force—as a rational instrument of policy."[5] This "old mode" of thinking, the bishops counter with an opposing conclusion: "The burden of proof remains on those who assert that meaningful limitation is present. . . . We hope that leaders will resist the notion that nuclear conflict can be limited, contained, or won in any traditional sense."

Dean Rusk is considerably more outspoken that the bishops:

> One does not know whether to be amused or alarmed by
> some of the precious and pseudosophisticated talk going
> around about strategies for limiting damage in a nuclear

war. It is suggested, for example, that counterforce strikes would send a signal to the other side that we would limit our strikes to military targets (in the hundreds) and that the other side would accommodate by leaving our cities alone. If the idea is to send signals, the best way to send a signal is to pick up the phone and talk to them. I have not seen anyone spell out how such a conversation would go. . . . Several hundred nuclear missiles aimed at "military" targets, with their accompanying cones of deadly fallout and the fatal pollution of the earth's atmosphere, cannot be distinguished from an all-out nuclear strike, except by playing with words unrelated to the real world. I have had enough experience with real crises to know that those carrying final responsibility are not going to confine themselves to scripts written in advance by think tanks. Anyone who thinks that an all-out Soviet attack on Western Europe, including the American conventional and nuclear forces stationed there, would not lead to an all-out nuclear war is living in a dream world.[6]

The old way of thinking about nuclear war is to say that its management and control is no different than the fine tuning of military strategy throughout the ages. What Secretary Rusk and the bishops argue is that armies having crossed the threshold of nuclear war on whatever basis, old precepts about war and rational policy no longer apply.

Fourth, the earlier discussion about thresholds, leads to an important question in normative thinking. The great American theologian Reinhold Niebuhr put forward the idea of moral thresholds. Up to the level of a certain threshold, moral choice proceeds in the realm of ambiguities and contradictions. Beyond the threshold, the moral issue becomes clearcut and moral choices involves not the balancing of relative goods and lesser evils but an unequivocal decision of right and wrong. For Niebuhr moral choice in civil rights in the 1950s and 1960s involved the moral threshold. When he proclaimed that if nuclear war broke out he hoped he would be among the first to die so that he would bear no responsibility for the retaliation and actions that followed, he placed nuclear war beyond the threshold. Where actions (nuclear war) or failures to act (civil rights) involve unacceptable moral consequences, the moral equation is fundamentally altered. In the bishops' words: "Nuclear weaponry has drastically changed the nature of warfare and the arms race poses a threat to human life and human civilization which is without precedent."

A fifth expression of a new mode of thinking in the bishop's letter appears in the section on "The Initiation of Nuclear War." In effect, the bishops join the four former American officials who in a celebrated article in *Foreign Affairs* magazine declared themselves for "no first use of nuclear weapons." The bishops are uncompromising in saying: "We do not perceive any situation in which the deliberate initiation of nuclear war, on however restricted a scale, can be morally justified." They call for meeting non-nuclear attacks, for example, an invasion of Western Europe by the Red Army, with "other than nuclear weapons." But they recognize that any transition from nuclear to non-nuclear defensive strategies will take time and the buildup of conventional forces in Europe. It would be helpful if the bishops had indicated how Europeans who have not responded to repeated appeals by American leaders for major increases defense expenditures would do so now.

The other controversy provoked by the no first use argument is that inspired by critics who ask what happens to the credibility of a deterrent if only one superpower has taken a serious self-denying pledge. Does a deterrent remain credible if one side promises it will never use it first? Would not an absolute prohibition involve the subordination of other values such as national survival and freedom to the single value of refraining from using nuclear weapons? What about the moral cost of failing to provide a nuclear shield for one's closest allies when it is the sole deterrent against military expansion of a superior power?

Finally, the prospects for peace in the world depend not on one approach but on trial and error in exploring many alternative courses. The stakes of survival are too large to justify leaders tying themselves to only one strategy of peace. Nor should negotiations be hedged in by preconditions. Secretary Rusk spoke out against the view that arms limitation talks require that the Soviets or we meet certain conditions saying: "Another bit of nonsense floating around these days is that we must expect far-reaching concessions from the Soviets before serious arms limitation talks can begin. . . . Some linkages are simply inescapable, but neither this country nor the Soviet Union is likely to pay for an admission ticket to let talks begin; the assumption must be that arms limitations can be in the interest of both sides, despite differences on other matters."[7]

The plain fact is that we have little to show from initiatives that have been taken in recent years. While earlier administrations can point to relatively successful SALT negotiations such as treaties barring nuclear weapons from the Antarctica, the ocean seabeds and orbiting in outer space; the Nuclear Test Ban Treaty of 1963 and the non-proliferation treaty, the present administration has little to show for its desultory, erratic and halting efforts. The Reagan administration could profit from the bishops urging that "negotiations should be pursued in every reasonable form possible" and the list of long-term and short-term objectives. George F. Kennan summarizes the proposals as "involving a whole series of arms control measures, including in effect a general stop to the arms race, deep bilateral cuts in arsenals, a comprehensive test ban treaty, and removal of the short-range weapons 'which multiply dangers disporportionate to their deterrent value.' It recognizes, however, that arms control agreements alone are insufficient if not accompanied by vigorous parallel efforts to reduce political tensions."[8]

Mr. Kennan's discovery that the bishops recognize the importance of negotiations to reduce political tensions narrows the differences they were seen as having with political leaders. In a letter to the *New York Times* on the bishop's letter under the heading "The Question Pure Moralists Have to Face," former President Richard M. Nixon wrote: "In the final analysis, of course, the question we all must address goes far beyond the control of production and deployment of nuclear weapons. Even if the Soviet Union and the United States agreed to cut their nuclear arsenals in half, we could still have a hell of a war if we failed to resolve those political differences that might result in armed conflict."[9] If President Nixon has a point it is that the relative emphasis on arms control and the quest for political settlements leads to the impression that the bishops are more aware of the urgency of the former than of the latter. They might wish to consider his advice that "we redouble our efforts to reduce our differences with the Soviet Union if possible. Where that is not possible, we must find ways to live with them rather than die over them."[10]

4. THE CHURCH AND ARMS CONTROL

As Mr. Rusk observed on another issue, a lot of nonsense has been floating around about the relationship of the church and politics. The bishops are careful to present their letter as a teaching document. They acknowledge that "not all statements in the letter have the same moral authority. At times we state universally binding moral principles found in the teaching of the church, at other times the pastoral letter makes specific applications which allow for diversity of opinion on the part of those who assess the factual data of situations differently." In a word, the bishops see the letter as a contribution to understanding, not as the final word, especially on technical and political problems.

It is surprising then that critics on the right and left should challenge the right of church leaders to speak out. The weight of organized groups addressing themselves to profoundly troubling issues can of course raise questions in the society. By what warrant do they speak? Apart from the fact that the bishops look out on the world from a more than 2,000 year tradition stretching at least from the Sermon on the Mount to the statements of Pope John Paul II, the participants represent a supremely well-qualified body of authorities in religion, morality and international relations. Father J. Bryan Hehir, the principal draftsman, would be a distinguished member of any international relations faculty anywhere in the world. Moreover, the letter, in contrast to so many other short-term collective efforts, is informed and inspired by the unity of a respected and enduring moral and political philosophy.

Father Hehir has praised the process above the product noting widespread public interest, organized discussions within the Catholic community spearheaded by groups such as the American Catholic Committee and dialogue in dioceses and parishes. Important as the aspects of the process may be, they hardly compare with the stunning success of hundreds of able leaders grappling for more than two years under some measure of collective discipline "to develop and perfect" what the authors called "a theology of peace suited to a civilization poised on the brink of self-destruction." The membership of the National Conference of Catholic Bishops under the chairmanship of Archbishop John R. Roach repeatedly discussed the two preliminary drafts. The Vatican sponsored several international esclesiastical sessions especially for European leaders.

Consultations went on with past and present governmental officials. A third draft was approved in early May, 1983, at a special meeting of the Conference in Chicago.

Looking back on the process and the product, Ambassador Kennan could say: "This paper . . . may fairly be described as the most profound and searching inquiry yet conducted by any responsible collective body into the relations of nuclear weaponry, and indeed of modern war in general, to moral philosophy, to politics and to the conscience of the national state."[11] It is a paper addressed to Catholics and non-Catholics alike. Its aim of sharing "the moral wisdom of the Catholic tradition with the larger society . . . and to participate in a common effort with all men and women of good will who seek to reverse the arms race and secure the peace of the world" could have far-reaching importance. The success of the effort should give heart to those who question the ability of religious bodies to launch and carry through such an enterprise. As a Protestant, I can only feel sorrow that a comparable effort has not been undertaken by the National Council of Churches.

For a peculiar combination of circumstances, the need has never been greater for studies such as the bishops' letter. Having often been criticized for its dogmatic inflexibility, the Catholic Church has become one of the more independent centers of inquiry. Its credibility is enhanced by making its assumptions explicit. Not every organizing group is as forthcoming. It is said that particular groups in the military and corporate sectors have come to play the dominant role in support of research and writing as their resources devoted to partisan think tanks and writers have burgeoned. Whatever its moral and intellectual commitments, the church today can afford a certain nonchalance on politics because its true beliefs transcend them. Its 2,000 year tradition of studying morality and politics and practicing diplomacy means that as an institution it stands alone.

There is something incongruous about saying that every other American institution—the military, corporations, or unions—are qualified to put forward individual and corporate views on right and wrong in foreign policy but religious groups must remain silent and aloof. Nor is it reassuring that only a narrow segment of military and corporate thinking is involved when favorite think tanks or scholars are generously funded to produce fairly predictable results. To deny bodies such as the Catholic Bishops an

opportunity to set in train a process as exacting as that which led to the bishops' letter would be tragic. Some powerful private and public leaders would have churchmen count angels on the end of a needle. By the bishops' letter, the church has demonstrated its competence in morality and foreign policy and the role of the church in serious reflections on arms control.

NOTES

1. Robert Osgood, CRIA Lecture at Charlottesville, Virginia, October 26, 1982.
2. George F. Kennan, "The Bishop's Letter," New York Times, May 1, 1983, p. E21.
3. *Washington Post,* October 1, 1981, p. A29.
4. *Ibid.*
5. Osgood, op. cit.
6. Rusk, op. cit.
7. *Ibid.*
8. Kennan, op. cit.
9. *The New York Times,* May 15, 1983, p. 20E.
10. Nixon, op. cit.
11. Kennan, op. cit.